BLOCKADE

During the summer and fall of 1971, the U.S. government supported the Pakistani military dictatorship while it massacred the people of East Bengal. But a group of Americans challenged this policy, tied up East Coast ports to Pakistani shipping, and had a major influence on changing U.S. policy.

Blockade is a story of the "nonviolent fleet" of canoes and kayaks that attempted to turn around the U.S. government.

BLOCK

ORBIS BOOKS
Maryknoll, New York 10545

ADE

A GUIDE TO
NON-VIOLENT INTERVENTION

RICHARD K. TAYLOR

Copyright © 1977 by Richard K. Taylor

Orbis Books, Maryknoll, New York 10545

All rights reserved

Printed in the United States of America

Library of Congress Cataloging in Publication Data

Taylor, Richard K
    Blockade

    Bibliography: p.
    1. Bangladesh—History—Revolution, 1971—Foreign
public opinion, American. 2. Public opinion—United
States. 3. Military assistance, American—Pakistan.
4. Passive resistance. I. Title.
DS395.5.T39   954.9'205   76-30600
ISBN 0-88344-036-9
ISBN 0-88344-037-7 pbk.

For my family
Phyllis, Debby, and Danny Taylor

CONTENTS

PREFACE

Candles cradled in their hands, two hundred Quakers moved south on Seventeenth Street toward the tumultuous western side of the White House. It was the evening of the May 1970 "New Mobe" demonstrations. One hundred thousand marchers had come to Washington to protest the American invasion of Cambodia.

The Quakers' inner light was also burning, fanned by a tense planning session earlier at the Florida Avenue Friends Meetinghouse. They hoped to witness for peace by an all-night march around the domain of the "Quaker" President, Richard M. Nixon. But they were strongly warned that they would never make it.

"You can't even get through DuPont Circle," a harrassed young medic reported. "There's tear gas and police all over the place." (I remember his tossled black hair and beard, the wild, exhausted look, the olive-drab army surplus cartridge belt with first aid boxes dangling, the white interne's coat with a red cross painted messily on the sleeve.) "The whole White House area is closed off," he puffed. "There are fires and property destruction at Georgetown University."

Uneasiness and uncertainty began to settle like fog among the meditating Quakers. Alternate routes to by-pass DuPont Circle were suggested. "Should we call off the whole thing?" Suddenly, a young Friend stood up and said:

"We're Quakers, aren't we?"

There was a mumble of irritated assent to such obviousness.

He pressed on. "We believe in following God's Spirit, don't we?"

Again, murmurs of assent.

"Then let's start to walk toward the White House. If we run into trouble, we can just stop and worship and ask the Spirit what to do."

All at once, the fumbling plans and groping seemed irrelevant. Reinvigorated by this reminder of their spiritual roots, the Quakers moved gravely from the Meetinghouse, lined up two-by-two, and started walking toward the White House. Phyllis, my wife, and I, who had been asked to help with the march, stepped toward the head of the line.

DuPont Circle smelled of tear gas, but was ominously quiet. Further south, however, the White House area was a battle zone. Searchlights caught running figures of angry demonstrators who had stayed behind after the end of the peaceful New Mobe rally. Tear gas grenades exploded. Acrid white clouds drifted under street lights. Police with gas masks and riot sticks moved slowly in small groups, then broke and ran after demonstrators.

We were halted by an imposing black policeman, with riot helmet, plastic face shield, and tear gas grenade belt. His face was tired but rock hard, and he held a billy club stiffly across his thighs.

"This area's closed. You can't go through."

"We're in a nonviolent demonstration for peace. We'd like to pass."

"If you move ahead, I'll either arrest you or gas you, depending on how much time I have."

We paused to absorb this unnerving bit of information, then said, "We'd like to ask God what to do."

With that we sat down on the sidewalk and sought the inner silence. Around us the cacophony of shouts, police radio squawks, and exploding gas grenades went on. As police looked on suspiciously, it seemed that the peace of God descended, a peace that both calmed and nudged. The outer discord continued, but somewhere deep inside a stirring, light, hush, calling touched the huddled Friends. Soon about half the group rose and walked to the same police-barricaded spot, lining up again, two-by-two.

"We'd like to go through."

"Like I said, the area's closed."

"We know you must be tired. You've probably been on duty all day. We don't have anything against you personally. But we feel that God is calling us to continue what we began."

"If you step off the curb, you'll either be gassed or arrested."

Cautiously, slowly, but decisively, we stepped off. To our surprise and joy, the policeman suddenly said, "O.K., come ahead." He stepped back and waved us through.

Like Joshua around the walls of Jericho, we circled the White House all night, pausing now and again for more silent waiting, sometimes having to move on because of tear gas. As we walked, we were joined by young demonstrators. At sunrise, on the Ellipse behind the White House, one showed me a gun he had brought with him. "I'm glad I stayed with you and didn't use this," he said.

If Yahweh is one who "works justice for the oppressed," as the psalmist declares, then it should have been no surprise to me to experience that prodding Presence so deeply at the White House. Nor should it have been a surprise to find it five years earlier, in Selma's little Browns Chapel Church and in the march to the Edmund Pettus Bridge with Martin Luther King and the black civil rights workers. And it was the same experience of the power and presence of God a decade later when the "People's Blockade" marched from a local church and planted a twelve-foot-high cross and Star of David on the railroad track of the Earle Naval Ammunition Depot, the track down which trains rumbled carrying bombs destined for Vietnamese homes and bodies.

It has been a continuing source of challenge and hope, of human love and divine incursion, to be a part of this movement of "satyagraha," of "truth force," of non-violent direct action—to picket innumerable super-markets in support of the farm workers, to slog through the mud of Resurrection City with the Poor People's Campaign, to keep vigil at the U.S.S.R. embassy in support of Soviet Jews, to march against the United Fruit Company in Costa Rica, to read the names of Vietnamese and American war dead on the Capitol steps.

Sometimes I'm terribly discouraged, awed by how little impact there's been on human cruelty. Yet I feel part of a tremendous historical force, made up of people seeking to overcome injustice without hating or killing their opponent.

Perhaps one reason why I take hope and do not simply look back with nostalgia on past involvements in peace and civil rights campaigns is that I am part of a continuing movement of men and women who are building a network of nonviolent training and action communities across America and in other countries. I also take hope in that experience of the nudging God who, it seems, "will not fail or be discouraged till he has established justice in the earth" (Isaiah 42:4).

The present book describes a particularly successful nonviolent campaign that grew out of this current movement. It took place in 1971, when the effort was just beginning.

INTRODUCTION

On July 14, 1971, a small group of people canoed into the oily waters of Baltimore harbor, trying to paddle in front of an in-coming Pakistani freighter. The news capsule in the next day's *Baltimore Morning Sun* read: "Police intercepted two canoe-loads of demonstrators and arrested seven persons attempting to prevent docking at Port Covington of the arms-laden Pakistani freighter Padma."

Eight thousand miles away, an avalanche of terrified refugees tumbled into India from East Pakistan. Most were Bengalis, who made up nearly all of East Pakistan's population. They carried with them memories of planes strafing villages, mass graves, bloated bodies floating down rivers, skeletons bleaching in the sun, women screaming as they were raped by West Pakistani troops.

Only eight months before, they had experienced the exaltation of a democratic election that promised constitutional rule, an end to dictatorship, and much greater autonomy for East Pakistan. But in March their hopes were crushed by a massive military action from West Pakistan, ordered by the governing dictator, General Yahya Khan. Before the struggle was over, more than a million Bengalis would be killed, twenty-five thousand women raped, and over nine million refugees would have fled to India.

Shocked by the first-hand report of a staff team describing a "reign of terror" by West Pakistani troops and the likelihood of famine in East Pakistan, most of the World Bank's major aid-giving nations quietly agreed to postpone indefinitely any new economic assistance to Pakistan.

One of the donor nations, however, the United States, stood out by continuing to send military and economic aid. In spite of recommendations from Kenneth Keating, U.S. ambassador to India, and East Pakistan consul Archer K. Blood (who reported "genocide" in his area), the U.S. government refused to condemn the West Pakistani action. The flow of American aid helped the army in its suppression and symbolically conveyed U.S. support for General Khan. As the release of secret government documents by columnist Jack Anderson later showed, the Nixon-Kissinger position was to "tilt" as strongly as possible in favor of West Pakistan's rampaging military regime.

What follows is the story of a nonviolent direct action campaign to educate the American people and turn around the American government. It tells of the Bengalis and Americans who worked to change government policy and to reveal what was happening, who felt the excitement, frustration, and fear of risk-taking action, and who experienced the satisfaction of seeing many of their goals achieved. The account is based on my own experiences in the campaign and extensive interviews with fellow participants as well as with police and others who viewed us "from the other side."

It has been impossible to give due credit to the two hundred or more people who took an active part in the campaign, picketing in the rain, getting sore feet in marches, paddling canoes under the bows of looming freighters, shivering all night in front of the White House, taking care of children and household tasks to free others for involvement. Rather I have sought to unfold the campaign through the eyes of a few people who were deeply involved and whose experience, I hope, reflects fairly the practicalities and the inner meaning of a strong nonviolent movement for social change.

Beyond the story of the "nonviolent fleet," I also speculate about how such campaigns apply to contemporary struggles for social justice, especially in the many situations where the United States violates its democratic values by ranging itself on the side of dictatorship and against the forces of human liberation. The campaign gives hope, I think, that we do not have to stand by helplessly, but can act forcefully and effectively to challenge such practices.

In these years of America's Bicentennial, we might do well to decide whether we want to continue aligning our nation with the rich and the powerful, the dictators and oligarchs of this world. If our identity is *not* with the King Georges of this earth, but with those revolutionaries who founded America, then we might find nonviolent struggle a potent contemporary means to reshape America toward the vision of political liberty and economic justice for all.

PART ONE

BLOCKADE!

*Fleeing the threat of violent death
in their homeland, thousands of East Pakistani refugees
in India meet a slower death in exile.
Near Calcutta, at one of the East Bengali refugee
camps, a woman is carried by her husband
to the hospital. She was dead on arrival.*

CHAPTER 1

A Base for Action

The newspapers that June carried photos of Bengali refugees with pleading eyes and emaciated faces. Word was leaking out of a massive and indiscriminate slaughter of human life as West Pakistani troops brutally crushed the political autonomy movement of the East.

During the summer of 1971, our lives were busy with plans to move to West Philadelphia to start a nonviolent training and action community, the Philadelphia Life Center. We had in mind a broader vision of building a nationwide movement of peace and social change activists, tentatively to be called the Movement for a New Society.

We wished that we could do something to respond to the carnage and the enormous need of East Pakistan's Bengali population. Work on the incipient Life Center was time-consuming, however, and we saw no real handle to take hold of the situation. It seemed a terrible tragedy, far from our shores, one that we were helpless to do anything about.

For eight years Phyllis and I had lived as a "nuclear family," having a homemade son, Danny, and then adopting a Korean-American daughter, Debbie. We had always been open to a more communal lifestyle, however, and were glad when our household was expanded

3

during 1970 and 1971 by three close friends, Ginny Coover, Bill Moyer, and Sue Carroll.

I had attended social work school with Bill, and I loved his raucous laughter and the humor always glinting in his eyes. He had a serious side too, and we used to go together to church groups to speak against the House Un-American Activities Committee's right-wing film, "Operation Abolition." Later, we both worked on the national staff of Martin Luther King's Southern Christian Leadership Conference. Ginny and I were the main organizers of Philadelphia support for SCLC's "Poor People's Campaign," shipping food, money, and people to Resurrection City in Washington. Sue and I helped put together the first "macro-analysis seminar," a study group aimed at understanding American society and thinking through ways to humanize it. Phyllis and I marched together in peace and civil rights demonstrations. She had begun to carve out a career, using her nursing training for social change in medicine.

At a June meeting of peace groups in Milwaukee, Bill was cornered by an old friend, Dick Murray. Dick had become friendly with Eqbal Ahmad, a Pakistani peace activist deeply concerned about the situation in East Pakistan. Ahmad told him that the United States was shipping military equipment and other aid to the murderous West Pakistani regime.

Dick kept pressing Bill with the question, "What can we do?" Bill finally asked how the U.S. aid is getting to Pakistan.

"By ship," was the reply.

Bill said, "How about somehow blockading the ships?"

"But the ships are coming to *East* Coast ports," Dick said. "You've *got* to do something." Bill remembers him as being very insistent.

When Bill returned to Philadelphia, he rejoined a half dozen of us who were doing a "macro-seminar" on the relation of the United States to Third World countries. On July 2 we met beneath an ancient chestnut tree in the courtyard between the American Friends Service Committee's downtown office and the barn-like red-brick bulk of Race Street Friends Meetinghouse.

As luck would have it, on the day of Bill's return, a seminar member was reporting on America's ties to Pakistan. It was pointed out that Pakistan is an important ally of the U.S. in South Asia and that the U.S. had been its major outside supplier. Over the years, we had built up their army with a billion dollars worth of military aid, supplying Sabre-jet fighters, light tanks, bombers, C-130 transports, guns, and ammunition. An arms embargo was imposed on both Pakistan and India from 1965 to 1967 because of the Indo-Pakistani border conflict, but many millions of dollars more of U.S. military aid was sent after the embargo was eased. Ironically, China had also been sending Pakistan some military aid, though not nearly as much as the United States.

U.S. economic assistance was also abundant, amounting to more than four billion dollars since 1954. We provided roughly half the country's total foreign aid, including amounts channeled through a ten-nation World Bank development consortium. The *New York Times* of May 30, 1971, said that the U.S. was committed to every phase of Pakistan's development, "as well as sustaining the nation's budget and currency."

Because of the nature of the August 1947 partition that separated Pakistan from India, the former country was divided into a Western and Eastern section, separated by 920 miles of Indian territory. Enormous differences also separated the two regions, differences in language, culture, and history. These were compounded by East Pakistan's well-documented belief that it was economically exploited by the Western section and under-represented in the nation's government.

The Awami League, a political party and people's movement, was born in East Pakistan in an attempt to rectify these grievances. Pakistan had been ruled basically by the military since 1958. A major goal of the Awami League was an end to dictatorial rule, the institution of democratic government, and greater autonomy for the East.

When elections for a national assembly were finally held in December 1970, the Awami League won a clear majority of the seats. Except for a few incidents, the election campaign and voting were held peacefully and all involved agreed the elections were both free and fair.

Negotiations about when to convene the assembly began, but the ruling dictator, General Khan, was obviously reluctant to move ahead. On March 25, he ordered the army to attack East Pakistan. The Awami League's leader, Sheikh Mujibur Rahman, was arrested, the League was banned, and the military began its ruthless suppression.

In our macro-seminar someone pulled out a June 22 article by *Times* reporter Tad Szulc. The story said that, although the U.S. State Department was claiming that all sales of military equipment to Pakistan had been banned since the Pakistani army began its repression in March, nevertheless Pakistani freighters were coming to U.S. ports and picking up military equipment. Bill added confirmation to this from his talks with Dick Murray in Milwaukee.

It broke in upon us that all the horror in East Pakistan was being perpetrated with the connivance of our own government. We were appalled. It was our bombers, fighters, tanks, and guns that were involved in causing all this suffering. It was our bullets that were killing the people who won the election.

What could we do? Someone said jokingly, "Mine the harbor."

Bill, thinking back to his Milwaukee conversations, said, "Use small boats. Mine the harbor with our bodies, ourselves. That would be the nonviolent way to do it."

At break time, I strolled over to the American Friends Service Committee lobby and noticed that a conference room was reserved for a consultation on Pakistan. Staff from various parts of the world would be there. Several of us had been on the AFSC staff or board and it was no problem to attend the meeting. We were disheartened, though, by the staff's response to our suggestion that a strong effort be made to stop U.S. support for the dictatorship and the war.

"We're working hard to get a fact-finding team into Pakistan," staff people said. "If we take a strong public position, it might cut off our ability to get entrance visas. Also, it might ruin our relationship with the Pakistani government. It could make it impossible to send in AFSC medical help and other aid the people need so desperately."

This seemed to us to be dealing more with effects than causes. Discouraged, we slumped back to the AFSC courtyard. The more we talked about "mining the harbor with ourselves," though, the better we liked the idea. Like civil rights sit-ins, it was dramatic, direct, and nonviolent. Potentially it could be picked up by the press and capture public attention. Using little boats to block a big freighter would paint a vivid picture that would stick in the public mind. It could give us a platform for informing people about the unjust U.S.-Pakistan relationship.

We knew from our civil rights experience that it is seldom enough for people to have "the facts." As Bill never tired of pointing out, everyone in the forties and fifties knew that black people in the South couldn't vote. But it wasn't until blacks began to march and picket to support their right to vote that the broader public became concerned and voting rights laws got onto the national political agenda. "Facts" have to become "news." People concerned about injustice have to stop giving lectures and start putting their bodies on the line. Robert Spike, a leading civil rights worker for the National Council of Churches, put it in theological terms when he said: "People's hearts are moved by a commitment that leads to suffering. That's a good part of the meaning of Christ's cross."

As our enthusiasm grew, Larry Scott, a white-haired peace worker who was sitting in on our seminar, spoke up. "I've been meeting with a group called Friends of East Bengal," he said. "It's made up of Philadelphia-based Bengalis and Americans. If you're going to start a nonviolent campaign, you should get in touch with them."

In the next few days, I made many calls to Washington to see if I could find out more about Pakistani ship schedules. Tom Dine, thirty-one-year-old legislative assistant to Sen. Frank Church, was particularly friendly and helpful. He and his wife, Joan, had lived in South Asia and had a deep feeling for the people there. He was strongly opposed to U.S. shipments to Pakistan. He told me he was sure other Pakistani ships would be coming in. Dale de Haan of Sen. Edward Kennedy's refugee subcommittee said, "We know that four or five Pakistan-registry ships will be touching at East Coast ports between now and August."

No one, though, seemed to have specific information—names of ships, ports of entry, dates of arrival. Mike Gertner, one of Senator Saxbe's aides, told us: "You can't get that information. It's classified. One of those Pentagon things."

I was both fascinated and frustrated by my phone conversation with Tad Szulc of the *New York Times*. He confirmed that four or five more ships would soon be sailing, but said he wouldn't be writing more articles like his June 22 story if the ships were carrying the same cargo.

"But why not report on continued military shipments," I asked, "particularly since the State Department is still saying they're not being sent?"

"It's just not news," he said brusquely. "There's no point in writing the same story over and over."

My ignorance of port operations was also very frustrating, but on Wednesday, July 7, I struck paydirt. After dead-end contacts with the Philadelphia Maritime Exchange and the Customs House, I stopped in at the Mercantile Library. The librarian immediately took me to the *Journal of Commerce,* a business newspaper with a lovely listing of ship arrivals and sailings. Within a few days, Fran Woods, a Roman Catholic nun who worked near the library and who shared our concern, was dropping in regularly to read the *Journal* and to call us with the expected arrival dates of Pakistani ships.

*At Camp Kalyani near Calcutta, a man
pleads with hungry East Pakistani refugees
clamoring for rice. They waited all day,
but the rice was never issued.*

CHAPTER 2

Friends of East Bengal

Sultana Krippendorff had been moved by a sense of desperate urgency for three months. Her family and friends lived in East Pakistan. The reports of massacre and rape chilled and sickened her. An excellent student, she had received her doctorate in communications from the University of Illinois in May. But she had read so many stories now of the systematic killing of doctors, lawyers, and other intellectuals, the machine-gunning of university students. Were she home now, she might be dead or fleeing for her life.

A *Newsweek* correspondent, visiting India's refugee-clogged border regions, wrote: "I have seen babies who've been shot, men who have had their backs whipped raw. I've seen people literally struck dumb by the horror of seeing their children murdered in front of them or their daughters dragged off into sexual slavery. I have no doubt at all that there have been a hundred My Lais and Lidices in East Pakistan—and I think there will be more."

New York Times correspondent Sydney Schanberg, before being expelled from Pakistan by the government, wrote: "The effluvia of fear is overwhelming."

Torn with the images of torture and death, terribly worried about family and friends, Sultana could hardly

11

keep her mind on her studies, her Philadelphia teaching job, or her new baby, Kaihan.

Her husband, Klaus, a communications specialist of German background, shared her deep concern. He put his skills to use by reprinting articles on the Pakistan bloodbath and distributing them to anyone who showed the slightest interest.

Sultana spent hours on the phone, pleading for help in her soft Bengali accent. "I got lists of individuals, peace groups, and politically-active organizations—SANE, the AFSC, Women's Strike for Peace, the Woman's International League for Peace and Freedom. They were all sympathetic," she said later, "but they were so occupied, so taken up with Vietnam. I found that many university professors with South Asia specialties were advisors to the State Department and weren't willing to get involved. Some people wrote letters to Congress, but nothing really seemed to click.

"At the end of April," she continued, "we pulled together the small group of Bengalis and Americans called 'Friends of East Bengal.' We were a bunch of naive people without much organizing experience. It seemed we could never get it together. We always had at least six dissents. We organized some teach-ins at the university, wrote letters, supported an information-lobbying group in Washington called the Bangladesh Information Center.

"Larry Scott was part of F.E.B. He suggested that you come to a meeting. On July 7 you and Bill walked in and took off on this wild scheme. We just sat there. It was so bizarre, so beyond every stretch of the imagination. To talk about trying to stop a ship. It was absolutely incredible.

"I had been involved in student politics and I was familiar with demonstrators screaming hatred and negating the opposition. I thought to myself, 'Do we really need one more U.S. group throwing rocks?'

"But you and Bill talked with a kind of professional

*Sultana Krippendorff
with her son, Kaihan.*

poise and conviction. You were introduced by Larry
Scott, whom everyone respected. And the symbolism of
ship-blocking was very chilling, very impressive. That's
why people listened and didn't fall over laughing. I don't
think anyone really believed you'd go ahead with it. To
have the action follow so quickly was amazing."

Bill and I came away from the meeting much encouraged. We had been given a free hand to set up a
Direct Action Committee for F.E.B. We sensed the
mixed feelings of the group, but we believed it would be a
vital source of information. We felt that many of the
participants would get involved in a well-conceived direct action campaign. We were sure too that many of the
people coming together to form the Philadelphia Life
Center, because of their strong commitment to nonviolent struggle, would join the Direct Action Committee.

Someone at the meeting had said, "If you're going to
try to stop ships, you'd better contact the longshoremen." I called Sultana and we spent July 8 and 9 giving
ourselves a quick course on the workings of the port of
Philadelphia. We tramped around the wharves and contacted officials in the Seafarers' Union, the Interna-

tional Longshoremen's Association, and the Maritime Union.

Sultana, with her flowing sari, petite figure, long black hair, lovely dark skin, and large brown eyes, made a strong impression and pleaded a persuasive case. We were pleased that these tough men of the docks responded sympathetically to the story of repression in East Bengal. John Resta, of the ILA's Clerks and Checkers, even invited us to the ILA's international convention in Miami, saying he would see that we were introduced to ILA president "Teddy" Gleason.

Bill Moyer's enthusiasm for the ship-blocking idea was growing. Questions were racing through his mind. Should we have a press conference soon? How about trying to load medical supplies on a ship? Should we start with picketing or go right into a blockade? What committees do we need?

On July 8 he received an exciting call from Charles Kahn, president of F.E.B. and a philosophy professor at the University of Pennsylvania. Word had been received that a Pakistani ship, the *Padma*, might dock in Baltimore on Sunday, July 11. Fran Woods said that, yes, the *Journal of Commerce* lists it.

A call to Dr. William Greenough, of the Bangladesh Information Center, confirmed not only that the *Padma* was coming, but that it carried a cargo of armaments. It had docked earlier in Montreal. Shipping agents had applied for a "hazardous cargo" permit, but had said no munitions or explosives were involved. "The ship is carrying foodstuffs and cobalt to be used in cancer treatment" was the official story. Suspicious Canadian officials, however, prodded by dockside picketers, discovered forty-six crates loaded with spare parts for F-86 Sabre-jet fighter planes. Canadian customs agents refused permission to load, seized the cargo, and suspended the exporter's license. The *Padma*, Dr. Greenough said, was heading for Baltimore.

A glance at a Baltimore map showed Fort McHenry

nestled on a point jutting into the harbor. In 1814, after a "perilous fight," the sight of Old Glory over its battlements inspired Francis Scott Key to write "The Star Spangled Banner." Bill and I called the Associated Press, United Press International, TV and radio stations in Philadelphia and Baltimore. Interest mingled with disbelief as reporters heard the news peg: "We're calling ourselves the Francis Scott Key Armada. We're going to blockade Baltimore harbor with a nonviolent fleet to prevent a Pakistani ship from docking. We're protesting U.S. support for genocide."

Elated with information on an actual ship arrival, the members of the Direct Action Committee met in a strategy session in our living room and listed on a flip chart all the tasks to be done. Committees were set up to handle such matters as recruitment, sign and leaflet-making, press contacts, and overall coordination. Training sessions were organized to do role-plays of possible nonviolent tactics. Special attention was given to developing lists of important mass media contacts and deciding on the best way to approach them. Individuals took responsibility for locating canoes, checking the police and legal situation, locating walkie-talkies, and coordinating transportation to Baltimore. John Johanning, a former philosophy professor who had just joined the Life Center, went to work making fifty posters to be carried in picket lines. Bengalis and Americans worked together on a recruitment committee and began calling a long list of peace activists, Quakers, F.E.B. contacts, and others who might be willing to come to Baltimore.

Dr. William Greenough, associate professor of medicine and chief of the infectious diseases division at Johns Hopkins University's School of Medicine had been part of a cholera research team in East Pakistan from 1962 to 1965 and had visited the land of Tagore three times between 1965 and 1971. His Bengali friends and other contacts gave him a unique source of information on the depradations being committed by West Pakistani troops. The conflict between what he knew and what the State Department was saying led him to help set up the Bangladesh Information Center to provide accurate information to Congress, the press, and all those wanting to influence the course of events. The Center's Washington newsletter soon became a key source of factual, eyewitness information. The Center also opened an office in Agartale, India, staffed by twenty-five volunteers, who distributed multivitamins to refugees and relayed first-hand information to Washington.

A tall, vigorous man, with an athletic build, wavy brown hair and pale blue eyes, Dr. Greenough cut an impressive figure as he moved from one congressional office to another, feeding in eyewitness accounts and position papers, getting experts to testify at congressional hearings, even preparing speeches for sympathetic senators and representatives. He was often joined by Dr. David Niven, who had also worked in East Pakistan, and by Anna Taylor, a beautiful Polish woman whose experience as a Belsen inmate during World War II had given her a deep feeling for refugees. Married to one of the cholera research doctors, Anna had on her own protested and fasted outside the Pakistani embassy and the White House. Later she became full-time staff for the Information Center.

One of the hardest things to fight was the official State Department position that the United States was not supporting or aiding General Khan's dictatorship. The Pentagon papers were starting to raise awareness that the Executive Branch would lie to Congress and the American people about Southeast Asia. But where were the concrete facts to counter State's position on Pakistan?

It was hard to argue against outright denials. For example, a State Department official said, on April 15, 1971: "No arms have been provided to the government of

Pakistan since the beginning of this crisis." On June 17, State told reporters: "No deliveries of military equipment have been made to Pakistan since March 25, when the fighting began."

An anonymous letter to Dr. Greenough, however, provided him with his own "Pentagon Papers." Included with the letter were secret Air Force documents —inventory statements listing arms being sent out on Pakistani ships. Within an hour of receiving the material, Dr. Greenough was on the move. He showed the papers to congressional aides and spent an afternoon discussing them with Tad Szulc.

This led to Szulc's June 22 article, "U.S. Military Goods Sent to Pakistan Despite Ban." Szulc described specific ships carrying U.S. military hardware to Pakistan. He mentioned the *Padma,* which, he said, was reported as carrying a cargo "that is said to include hundreds of thousands of pounds of spare parts and accessories for planes and military vehicles." Confronted with these facts, senior State Department officials admitted that at least two ships were headed for Pakistan carrying "foreign military sales items." "Officials appeared to be at a loss to explain the shipments in the light of the official ban," Szulc wrote.

It was a fantastic stroke to cut through the government's evasions, but Dr. Greenough and others at the Information Center felt frustrated after the story broke. What should they do next? How could they keep the story visible? Working with Senator Church's legislative assistant, Tom Dine, they had drafted legislation to cut off military and economic aid to Pakistan. But without a constant flow of news to keep the issue hot and in front of Congress, the legislation would die in committee.

It was while these discussions were going on that Jack Patterson called Dr. Greenough about the nonviolent fleet. "It sounded a little crazy at first," Dr. Greenough admits, but he made a note to attend the planning meeting at Stony Run Friends Meetinghouse on Sunday, July 11.

Jack Patterson, a tall, slim, mustached, thirty-two-year-old peace secretary for Baltimore's AFSC office, is an inveterate magazine and newspaper reader, and he had learned a lot about what was happening in Pakistan. The conflict seemed to him like David and Goliath, where David probably didn't even have a slingshot. A phone call from Bill Moyer gave him an opportunity to act. Within a few hours, he became one of the key Baltimore contacts. He secured Stony Run Meetinghouse (a building owned by Baltimore Quakers) as a place where demonstrators could sleep, cook, and have meetings. He compiled lists of potential demonstrators and started recruitment calls. And he began to check out specific sources of information on just when and where the *Padma* would arrive.

A phone call about the nonviolent fleet came at just the right time for Alex Cox, a red-haired Texan and guidance counsellor in the Philadelphia school system. He had just returned from the National Education Association convention and his summer was relatively free. "That whole policy of providing arms to Pakistan, putting our tax money into supporting military factions—it made me sick. The blockade seemed an imaginative way to dramatize to the American public what was happening."

Working on a barn in the Philadelphia suburbs, Wayne Lauser was equally glad to get involved. A twenty-three-year-old peace activist, who in 1969 had made a dramatic walk from Cleveland to Washington to put his draft card on Defense Secretary Laird's desk, Wayne was waiting for sentencing for draft resistance. An avid outdoorsman, hiker, and backpacker, Wayne felt that his canoeing skills would be useful in the blockade.

Growing up in a Quaker peace activist family, twenty-four-year-old Sally Willoughby had been involved in antimilitary demonstrations since she was a child. In the summer of 1971, she was living in a peace workers' commune and had just returned from a sailboat trip to Cuba, sponsored by the War Resisters League. Carrying children's art work from all over the United States, the trip was a people-to-people mission cutting through the U.S. trade embargo. The proposed blockade looked to Sally like an effective way to bring a horrible situation to public attention.

Things were more complex for Mal Scott, a Quaker and an intergroup relations staff person for the Philadelphia schools. What about his children? The house he and his wife, Barbara, lived in was constantly ringing with the noise of preschool, junior high, and high school kids—Mal's own from a previous marriage, a stepdaughter, two black foster children, and innumerable friends who loved Scott's adventuresomeness and free-swinging ways. But it sounded to Mal like the right thing to do.

"Besides," he recalls, "it was my time. I hadn't been arrested for two years, since some civil rights sit-ins."

The kids were eager to participate. Alexandra Scott, a junior high student on vacation from the Arthur Morgan School in North Carolina, said it was disgusting that the United States was secretly providing arms, and besides, it was such an adventure that she just had to go. Fifteen-year-old Molly McMullin thought it sounded exciting and her sister, Priscilla, was talking about going. Finally, Mal piled his own children and several friends into a large van and headed for Baltimore.

*Two kayaks from the nonviolent fleet
return from "maneuvers" in Baltimore harbor.*

CHAPTER 3

The Pursuit of the Padma

The Baltimore Morning Sun, Sunday, July 11, 1971

AGNEW GOES ROUND WORLD
TO REASSURE RIGHTIST ELITES
[front page headline]

WORLD BANK DIRECTORS
TOLD EAST PAKISTAN IS IN CHAOS
[front page headline]

The local population remains in a
state of extreme terror because of
the harsh regime introduced by
President A.M. Yahya Khan's
West Pakistani troops." *[from the
news story]*

SHIPPING IN THE PORT OF BALTIMORE
—Wednesday—Padma (Pak.)—East-West Shipping Agency" *[business section]*

Hammering down Route 95 from Philadelphia to Baltimore, we smiled at one another as we looked back and
saw the other cars with canoes and kayaks strapped to

baggage racks. Bill flipped on the radio as we approached Baltimore. Almost immediately we heard a news announcer say: "Today a Pakistani freighter will attempt to dock in the harbor, but a group from Philadelphia, calling themselves 'Friends of East Bengal,' intend to block it with small boats."

It occurred to us that, with the growing publicity about our intentions, authorities might want to shut down information on the *Padma*'s schedule. And indeed, when we arrived at the tree-shaded Stony Run Meetinghouse, Jack Patterson and Dr. Greenough told us that there was no word as yet on the *Padma*'s arrival.

The meeting drew over one hundred people, many recruited through Baltimore Quaker and peace organization contacts, but also a sizeable American and Bengali contingent from Philadelphia and a dozen Bengalis from New York City. Later, Charles Fager, a Quaker writer and newspaperman, arrived from Boston with his brother.

Rumor had it that the ship would be docking at Pier 8, Port Covington, a section of the waterfront where the Western Maryland Railroad had an enormous gray warehouse. We contacted press, radio, and TV, then drove to the area, parked cars along the chain-link fence guarding the warehouse, and set up a ninety-person picket line near the gate.

Near Pier 8 was a large vacant lot extending to the harbor waters. From there we made the first launch of the Francis Scott Key Armada, pushing a tiny rubber raft, an aluminum canoe, and a one-person "Seafish" sailboat through the green-purple-lavender oil slicks into the opaque brown water. Bengalis had a new name for East Pakistan, and as the flotilla pushed off, an excited Bengali doctor from Johns Hopkins University shouted, "You are first Navy of Bangladesh!"

Curious TV reporters took films of the boats and the picket line. Charles Walker, director of field studies for

*A canoe from the nonviolent fleet tries
to get past Coast Guard cutters to blockade the Padma.*

Haverford College's Nonviolent Action Research Project, told them: "We're calling this phase of the action 'The Pursuit of the *Padma.*' Our nonviolent fleet will find just where it's going to dock and how we can best position ourselves to block it."

One reporter angrily confronted Bill Moyer: "You got us here on a wild goose chase. The boat's not here. You must have lousy information. Do you feel bad about your futile effort?"

Bill smiled: "I guess you don't know a successful blockade when you see one. The ship is afraid to come in. We're claiming success and we're going to continue. We'll be back tomorrow."

Both the NBC and CBS TV channels that night had excellent coverage of the Pakistan story and our action. One station described what had happened in the invasion and showed footage of hungry, disease-ravaged Bengali refugees in India. Then it devoted a full five minutes to our picket, the nonviolent fleet, and an interview with a Bengali demonstrator with his head turned away from the camera for fear that his family in Bangladesh would face retaliation were he recognized.

We were jubilant. Ours was the top news story of the evening. The message was starting to get across.

The Baltimore Morning Sun, Monday, July 12, 1971

KISSINGER LEAVES PAKISTAN
AFTER MEETINGS WITH YAHYA

SHIP'S DELAY THWARTS
PAKISTAN ARMS PROTEST

Demonstrators launched three small boats yesterday in the harbor to 'search' for the expected vessel. . . . Dr. William Greenough. . . said the group would maintain a vigil until the ship arrives. . . . Demonstrators. . . included Pakistani women in colorful saris and Bengali sailors who had jumped ship to prevent reprisals against them.

We telephoned the Coast Guard on Sunday evening and were told that the *Padma* would not arrive until Wednesday. They were obviously beginning to get suspicious of our calls, however, and this was the last definite information they shared with us.

A person on the other end of the line at the Baltimore Maritime Exchange said: "Yes, we keep all information on in-coming ships. The *Padma?* Er ... er ... No! We don't know about it."

Newspaper reporters' curiosity had been piqued, however, and they often called us to find what we knew and to give us the latest information or, more likely, the latest rumor. They sensed that some sort of major confrontation was in the works, and they wanted to be sure to be on top of the story.

As Jack Patterson later reflected: "We turned each postponement into an advantage. Everyone was getting caught up in asking, 'Where's the *Padma?* Where's the *Padma?*' Ironically, the big news became, 'It's still not here!' "

Bill and Jack regularly checked the newspapers, the Maryland Port Authority, and the Bay Pilots' Association. The Association provides pilots to bring sea-going ships through the narrow harbor channel. We were surprised and pleased to find that they readily gave us information on the *Padma*'s expected arrival. But suspicion and rumors abounded, and we wondered if the ship might slip in without our knowledge. Some Bengalis even set up a ship lookout on Hawkins Point, which protruded into the harbor, hoping they could identify the ship if all our information sources shut down completely.

Quakers from Stony Run became very interested in the action. They allowed us to sleep at the meetinghouse and to use their phone, meeting rooms, and office space. We kept finding more and more food that Meeting members quietly dropped off at the kitchen.

Our Sunday night strategy session at the meeting-house focused both on recruiting demonstrators for the long haul (we had been expecting a weekend action, and many people had left) and on thinking through meaningful actions for the next three days to keep the issue in the public eye. East-West Shipping Agency, the Baltimore company handling the *Padma*, seemed a likely focus. We mimeographed leaflets saying that the *Padma* would not even come into the port if the shipping company would take a stand against the destruction of human life and refuse to handle the vessel.

Walter Spieker, vice president and general manager of East-West Shipping Agency, found himself on Monday morning with fifteen pickets in front of his office and two representatives waiting to talk to him. A glance at the *Padma*'s manifest told him that no arms were being loaded in Baltimore. His New York office assured him that there were no arms on the ship. He had not seen the New York manifest, and documents, of course, can be falsified. Since the shipping company doesn't inspect the crates, he couldn't speak with complete certainty. But he told Jack Patterson and Diana Schramm, who left the picket line to negotiate with him, that he was convinced no arms were aboard.[1] He also let drop that the *Padma* was expected on Wednesday.

"I was caught," he remembers feeling. "Everything was concentrated on East-West Shipping—picketers, the press. I was neutral as regards the situation in Pakistan. Later I got a call from a trucker who said he had a shipment from an army depot for the *Padma*. I told

---

1. Surprisingly, the July 15 *Baltimore Sun* carried a State Department release saying that the cargo included an arms shipment with such items as $924,329 worth of spare aircraft parts, spare parts for military vehicles valued at $184,187, and $70,000 worth of other military equipment. The statement said the export license for the shipment was issued before the March 25 ban on military cargoes.

him not to come, to turn around. Here I was making statements to the press and the dockworkers' union about no arms being loaded. I didn't want any arms going near that ship."

On leaving East-West Shipping, demonstrators marched over to the Federal Building and visited the offices of Baltimore congressmen, describing the situation and urging support for legislation to cut off U.S. aid to the dictatorship. Television and newspapers again covered the demonstration, reinforcing our feeling of having found a way to keep the issue before the public. At the evening strategy meeting, plans were laid for a demonstration at the U.S. Customs House to demand that the government inspect the crates to be loaded.

The Baltimore Morning Sun, Tuesday, July 13, 1971

EAST PAKISTAN 'TERROR' CITED

A World Bank mission in a secret report paints a picture of East Pakistanis living in terror of President Yahya Khan's army and stalked by the specter of starvation.

SHIPPING AGENT IS TARGET OF PAKISTAN ARMS PROTEST

A blockade of the Port Covington Terminal by [the demonstrators'] 'nonviolent navy' is still scheduled for tomorrow.

Sultana Krippendorff slowly had been drawn into the picketing and marches. Her fears about screaming, rock-throwing demonstrators had all but disappeared.

"Communications is my field," she reflects, "and I was

tremendously impressed by the respect you commun-
icated to the other side—police at the demonstrations,
the shipping agents, even the West Pakistanis you
wrote about in your leaflets and press releases. You
didn't put the blame on any individual. You treated
them as enslaved in a system and you were trying to
include them. You didn't use anger or sarcasm, even
when on-lookers at demonstrations shouted negative
remarks. Instead of accusing, you pointed to a larger
morality beyond all of us in which all should be interested.

"I remember Bill Moyer, at the Quaker Meeting's
cramped little office, asking me if I wanted to make calls
to the press. I said, 'I'm embarrassed. I've never done
this before. How do I do it?' He replied, 'Just convince
yourself that you're morally right. Then you'll be able to
convince them.'

"Our marches and pickets were always quiet and dig-
nified. Police could see that we weren't rabble-rousers
and wouldn't go haywire. Yet the actions weren't passive. They were more active, in terms of communication,
than if we'd gone into an orgy of throwing rocks.

"When I first joined the demonstrations, I thought,
'What kind of ludicrous situation am I in?' But the funny
thing for me was not just doing these outrageous things,
but getting over my embarrassment, being able to go up
to people on the street and hand them a leaflet and
explain my concern.

"I began to see that it was effective. Not only did
people stop to look and ask questions, but the press took
us seriously, never poked fun at us, never treated us as
off the deep end. Instead of just expressing pent-up
anger and frustration, we were able to communicate a
moral statement—people are being killed, Americans
are involved, we have to act. We created an event that
made this into news."

Sultana was moved too by the commitment of foreign-
ers to a situation where they had no self-interest. Peo-

BILL MOYER LEADS PICKET LINE AT THE PORT IN BALTIMORE.

ple were working eighteen hours a day on the campaign,
sitting in strategy sessions, preparing signs, leaflets,
and press releases, calling the TV stations, recruiting,
demonstrating. Sometimes it felt like a mechanical process had been set in motion that couldn't be halted.
Sultana was reminded of Gandhi stories: "moral purists,
with heads bloodied by police clubs, going like lemmings
into the ocean."

"The drama gave it enormous momentum," Jack Patterson said later. "It was like a tar-baby. Once you got stuck, it tended to involve you completely."

Bill Moyer had a tough time keeping his mind on the Customs House demonstration. He had been interviewed on both radio and TV, so the story was still hot, but information on the *Padma* was getting scarce. Broenning Park, with its small boat ramp near the South Baltimore General Hospital, had been picked as the best launch site for the nonviolent fleet. But it would take a half-hour to paddle from there to the Pier 8 channel, so it was crucial to have enough advance warning to get everyone in place and the boats into the water. Could it be that we would put out all this effort and miss the big event, the *Padma*'s arrival?

"There are hundreds of rumors," Bill wrote in his journal on July 13. "People are panicky about where the *Padma* is, when it'll get here."

East-West Shipping's office said it would come in Wednesday afternoon. The Coast Guard talked vaguely about 9 P.M. Wednesday. The longshoremen had heard Thursday morning. The Maritime Exchange claimed not to know anything. A Port Authority man said he wasn't sure it would come to Baltimore!

Dave Martin and some Bengali sailors who had jumped ship from the *Padma* on an earlier voyage positioned themselves on Hawkins Point, ready to run to a nearby phone booth at first sight of the ship. Newspaper reporters searched piers and phoned in to compare notes. A pilot pick-up had not yet been scheduled, the Bay Pilots reported at 11:40 P.M. Around midnight, however, a UPI reporter called to say he had definite word the *Padma* would arrive sometime Wednesday.

*Mal Scott's family and friends
put together the foldboats that will be part
of the nonviolent fleet.*

CHAPTER 4

The Nonviolent Fleet in Action

The Baltimore Morning Sun, Wednesday, July 14, 1971

EDITORIAL

The U.S. actions [regarding Pakistan] thus far have been inadequate and unsatisfactory. Economic help is being extended through the Pakistan government and licenses for exports of arms to Pakistan, which were issued before March 25, are being honored, although such shipments are being protested in the U.S. and in other countries. ... The tragedy is already immense and is still growing.

Bill was on the phone by 7 A.M. He noted that the weather was to be sunny, high in the eighties, a 10 percent chance of rain. The Bay Pilots still had no word of the *Padma* and casually dropped the disconcerting news that the ship might not use a pilot from their agency. The Coast Guard and Maritime Exchange claimed no word on the ship, but a *Baltimore Sun* source said it definitely was coming to Pier 8.

Assuming that we would probably launch the fleet, at least as a precautionary measure, Bill called Sergeant Rawlings of the police division covering the Broenning Park area. "I explained our purpose and told him we'd be nonviolent. I said that meant that if anyone started trouble, we'd protect the police, stand in front of them. He replied, 'In all my thirty years on the force, no one has said anything like that.' I couldn't be sure, but it sounded as though he was semi-crying."

Capt. Francis X. Hayes was also up early. As commander of the Tactical Section of the Baltimore City Police, he had a formidable force at his disposal: helicopters, a riot squad, an emergency vehicle unit, a bomb disposal unit, and the K-9 corps. Today, however, he decided to place his specially trained tactical patrolmen, who had handled many antiwar and civil rights demonstrations, on three Coast Guard cutters and two large police boats used by the Marine Police. Others would be stationed on shore to handle any demonstrations there.

He would work closely with Sergeant Duffy, a Marine policeman with over twenty years on the force. From the fifty-foot, steel-hulled police launch, the *Intrepid*, with its two diesel engines putting out 640 horsepower and 24.7 mph top speed, they would be in a good position to oversee the operation.

They had decided to form a wedge of police and Coast Guard boats to keep the demonstrators from the *Padma*, which would come up the Patapsco River through the Brewster Channel, then into the Fort McHenry Channel and on into Pier 8 through the Ferry Bar Channel. Just in case, a Coast Guard fireboat was kept on alert.

Captain Hayes was determined to enforce the law, but he was also concerned for the demonstrators' safety. A big freighter could cut a canoe in half. It would take the length of a football field to stop its forward motion. The wake of the freighter could capsize the small boats. And the ship's prop? "Why, those big propellers would cut

them up like ground beef," the captain remembers
thinking.

He instructed his men to watch out for the demonstrators' safety. "We'll have to make arrests if they en-
danger themselves," he said.

I've canoed Wyoming's Snake River, Missouri's Current, the Delaware in Pennsylvania, the East Branch of
the Penobscot in Maine, and innumerable lakes and
streams. There's a special smell that fresh white water
makes as you plunge through the waves, dodging boul-
ders and trying not to get swamped. I love to canoe, but
as I stood in Broenning Park, I thought to myself, "This
certainly isn't the kind of place I'd *prefer* to paddle
around in."

South Baltimore General Hospital stood majestically
on a green-lawned hill overlooking the harbor, but here
by the shore were orange peels, an "Old Taylor" whiskey
bottle, bent soda cans, plastic milk cartons, a soggy old
slipper, thirty bald tires washed up on dirty, barnacle-
encrusted rocks—all the flotsam and jetsam of an indus-
trial harbor meant for tugboaters and ship captains
rather than nature-happy canoers.

A wide river came in sluggishly from the left, carrying
an old tire in its murky brown waters. There was a
rotten smell—a dead fish?—by the edge. A stream of
morning traffic growled across a bridge three hundred
yards to our left. Dump trucks squeaked and bounced on
a roadway a hundred feet behind us.

Across the river stood high concrete silos with the
words "Marquette Cement Company" in large black letters on the side. Behind a long, gray-metal warehouse
and around a point of land was Pier 8 Port Covington.

Red buoys and black posts marked the river channel
to the harbor, which lay magnificently glistening in the
sun to our right. A mile across it I could see enormous
freighters docked at piers and cranes and derricks,

creaking faintly, loading and unloading cargoes. A tugboat chugged importantly past us, its wake throwing a
plastic bread wrapper higher up on the shore. Heavy
machinery from a factory across the river made a low-
hummed puff and whine, like a whale blowing.

What fascinated the fifty or so gathering "armada"
members, however, was the large police boat, its powerful engine throbbing, positioned just off shore in front of
the park's concrete launch ramp. "The *Intrepid*—what
an appropriate name," someone commented.

Other police drove up in patrol cars and observed us as
we unloaded canoes. Watching them, I felt a familiar
knot in my stomach. "Will they try to stop us? Can they
ruin it?" flashed through my mind. Several people
strolled over to talk to them, trying to reassure them
about our open and nonviolent intentions. Off and on,
dialogue with the police continued for the better part of
the morning.

Newspaper reporters slouched in their cars, waiting
for the action. Lee and Alexandra Scott and their two
black foster brothers, Kevin and Clarence Knowles,
spent over an hour figuring out how to put together the
frame and canvas of two borrowed foldboats. Mal Scott
padded around in bare feet, shirtless and in blue walking shorts, working on the foldboats and enjoying the
warm July sun. Nervousness had its effect, and people
made repeated trips to the South Baltimore Hospital's
bathrooms.

Many of the demonstrators had been with us since
Sunday, but others had driven down from Philadelphia
only that morning. At about ten o'clock, I called the
group together to bring newcomers up to date and discuss plans. I said that our purpose was to put a public
spotlight on U.S. support for the Pakistani dictatorship
and to try with our own bodies to prevent the ship from
docking.

"To me, this ship represents twenty million lives," I
said. "That's how many people may die or be made home-

less in Bangladesh if we don't change things." (Jack Patterson remembers listening and feeling that the *Padma* "seemed like evil incarnated in a piece of steel.")

I explained that arrests were likely if we actually got into the channel. We could be charged with violating maritime and possibly other laws. I said that everyone was encouraged to participate. Those who didn't feel ready or able to be arrested could play an important role by forming a vigil line along the roadway, carrying signs and handing out leaflets, or by paddling canoes and staying out of the shipping lane. For those ready to be arrested (and I was glad to see more than a dozen hands go up when I asked who would risk jail), we would try to form a line of boats across the channel in front of Pier 8.

Charlie Walker, standing at the edge of the meeting, reminded himself how nonviolent activists sometimes naively believe that whatever violence does materialize will be like TV violence—bloodless, purely visual, "and afterwards the actors go home with the ketchup washed off." But in a situation where tiny craft take on a large ship, with armed police in a strange situation, serious injury and even a fatality couldn't be ruled out. He talked to the volunteers to be sure they realized the risks.

Wayne Lauser, tall, with a head band, steel-rimmed glasses and sleeves rolled up, stood out in the crowd. Like Charles, he was thinking about the risks. "I started seeing the confrontation in my mind," he remembers. "I started imagining being out there, only a foot above the water, looking up at the on-coming bow of the freighter. For the first time, I realized the ante we were putting up. I hadn't come down to give my life for this witness, and I asked myself, could I take that chance? My personal answer finally was, yes, if the risk's there, I'll have to accept it."

Speaking slowly and seriously, Wayne asked the group to look at the same picture, to face the danger. He talked about the turbulence of a large ship, how long it takes to stop, the tremendous amount of water it sucks under its bow, the possibility of being pulled into the screws. He also went over some basic canoe safety —wear lifejackets, stick together, everyone help if someone overturns. He tried to present it so people would have space to say, "No, I don't want to do this."

At the end of the meeting, we told reporters that we still weren't sure when the *Padma* would arrive, but we were going to paddle to Pier 8 "for maneuvers."

"We're not familiar with the harbor waters," we said, "and we want to test our tactics and see if we have trouble with currents or wind."

As we readied our craft for the launch, however, a police officer came up. He told Charlie Walker, our "beach coordinator," that park regulations forbid launching without permit.

"You'll be arrested," he said, "if you put boats in the water."

Charlie, who has been in dozens of demonstrations, sensed that the police felt they had to perform ritualistic roles—saying certain things for the record, but not really stopping us. He encouraged people to go ahead with the launch.

A small crowd gathered near the police. People argued that fishermen had told us they launched from this spot without a permit. The police admitted they'd made no arrests in such circumstances, but, insisting that our launch would violate "Park Rule No. 51," they formed a line between us and the water. The arrival of a police paddy wagon emphasized their seriousness.

While we talked, Charles Kahn called the park office and was told that no permission could be given over the phone. The office, he was informed, would be closed till mid-afternoon. A worried Dr. Greenough tore off in his car to see if any nearby marinas would let us put into the water from their docks. Charles Kahn dragged his orange rubber raft near the water to see what the police would do. They took his name and read him his rights, so he backed off and came back to the group looking discouraged.

This was a confrontation we hadn't expected. If we didn't try to launch, there would be no way to get to the *Padma*, but if we were all arrested on the shore, then we'd be in the same bind. We felt stuck, and nerves began to fray.

I had seen a little marina, the Ladybug, up-river beyond the bridge. I told the group I'd take one canoe and try to launch from there. That would put at least one boat in the water. If I was successful and the police remained adamant here, others could come to the Ladybug for the launch.

Two other members of the fleet and I lashed a canoe to a car and drove to the marina, wondering if the police would follow us or if the owner would keep us out. We whipped into the parking lot, took off the canoe, and put it into the water, steering between some old, splintered pilings and an ancient barge.

When we paddled under the bridge, we were surprised to see the whole "fleet" of three kayaks, two canoes, and a rubber raft paddling bravely offshore near the *Intrepid*. For Wayne Lauser the tip-off for getting into the water had come when he saw a TV camera crew arrive.

"I realized that whoever tried to launch would make a statement, whether they were arrested or not," he recalls. "I asked Sally Willoughby and Stephanie Hollyman if they were willing to try a launch, and they immediately said they were. We told the police we were going ahead, then picked up a canoe, carried it over to the ramp, and began stowing lifejackets and gear."

The police came over and took their names.

"You'll be arrested as soon as the canoe touches the water," they said.

Wayne told them, "You have to do what you have to do, but we came here to witness against arms for Pakistan, and we're going to do that."

Wayne and Sally picked up the canoe and put it in the water. As Wayne got in, an officer read them their rights. They pushed off, expecting at any moment to be siezed.

"But then the three of us looked back and there were the police and our friends. There was a spontaneous cheer from the shore, and then the other boats were launched. The police just stood and watched."

The whole fleet paddled over to Pier 8, stopping occasionally near rusting barges and abandoned piers to get a feel for the situation. The *Intrepid* tailed along at a respectful distance, the police on deck observing us. We felt out of place in a world designed for huge ships and scurrying tugs. A freighter would pass quite far from us, out in the shipping lane, and we'd bob up and down in its wake like empty pop bottles a few minutes later. But there was also a sense of real joy at being on the water, smiling at one another, sweating with the strokes, using our muscles after the suspenseful waiting on the shore. Alex Cox remembers feeling reassured that the water was calm and his canoe responded well. Fifteen-year-old Molly McMullin, her long hair tossed by the breeze, recalls that she felt "beautiful, free, and good."

Pier 8, Port Covington, is an imposing set of wharves, rising thirty or forty feet out of the water. Between them is a rectangular body of water, as big as two football fields, where two ships can dock at once. We tried several blocking formations, finally settling on a straight line of canoes and kayaks directly across the mouth of the pier's entrance.

But there was no sign of the *Padma*. Bill called us from the shore with a walkie-talkie and said the Bay Pilots were predicting a night arrival. After an hour of "maneuvers," we stroked back to the park, worn-out, sunbaked, and hungry.

Back at Stony Run, we were just heating a six o'clock supper when the phone rang and a newspaper reporter said he had definite word the *Padma* was on its way into the harbor. The meetinghouse became a fire station when the fire bell rings. We had left boats on top of our cars, so we were heading back to the park within seconds. We tore through downtown Baltimore, screeched up to the park, and launched three canoes and two kayaks with no ceremony.

The water was choppier now, and the sun was getting low. The *Intrepid* was there to greet us, but now it was backed up by another police boat and three Coast Guard cutters. Sergeant Duffy's bullhorn-amplified voice boomed across the water: "Come over here. I want to talk. You're in danger. Who's your leader?"

"We don't have a leader," I shouted, paddling hard like the rest toward Pier 8. "You'll have to talk to all of us."

"I've been in this business twenty years," came Duffy's authoritative voice. "The wakes of these freighters are enormous. You can be flipped over and chopped up by their propellers. Go over to the side, out of the channel, and you can peacefully protest."

"You have to do what you have to do," I called back, paddling doggedly, "but we're here to try to block the *Padma*."

The *Intrepid* had to gun its engine and come about. Sergeant Duffy's voice became more impatient: "You're violating harbor regulations by blocking a shipping lane. You'll be arrested if you don't get out of the way."

Looking beyond the police flotilla, we could see silhouettes of freighters, docks, and cranes against the far shore and, just to their left, the smaller outline of a white-hulled freighter and its tug escort, now far away, but closing fast. Clearly it was the *Padma*, getting bigger by the minute. We paddled hard through the swells and wind, fearful of not getting to the pier in time. Paddles smacked the tops of waves and spray splashed aboard. The *Padma*'s horn let out a deafening blast, an urgent warning to get out of the way.

A large white yacht from the Ladybug Marina roared

ALEX COX, IN STERN, PADDLES IN FRONT OF THE S.S. PADMA.

up, loaded with reporters. A smaller inboard, steered by
a television reporter with her camera crew clinging pre-
cariously in the back, sped in for a closer look. The
churning Coast Guard thirty-footers, each with a blue-
uniformed policeman standing in the back, began to
edge between us and the pier.

Mal Scott recalls that he had faith that the *Padma*
wouldn't run him down. He realized, though, that he and
his daughter might not even be seen by the ship's pilot if
they got under that giant bow. Still, he bent his powerful
six-foot four-inch frame into the double-bladed paddle
and sent the kayak scuttering across the water toward
the channel.

"I didn't fully realize the danger we were in till we
were near the dock," Alexandra Scott, then twelve years
old, remembers. "The workmen on the dock were yelling
for us to get the hell out of there, that the ship was not
stopping and we were going to go down like ants from
the suction. I was in the kayak with my dad, and for the
first time in my life I felt tiny. I felt so small compared to
that ship. I started getting scared, but I saw the TV
camera boat and I realized we were actually making a
point. I'd been afraid no one would know and nothing
would come of our efforts.

"The monster came closer and closer. We dodged,
weaved, and paddled like hell. It was a mad frenzy, like a
strange game of tag—all our boats moving around like
snakes, and the stupid, huge power police boats trying to
catch us with their grappling hooks. We almost had
them beaten until they mushed us between two cutters
and just pulled us on board their boat."

Alexandra's friend, Molly McMullin, a sophomore at
Germantown Friends School, remembers wanting to get
out of there as soon as possible. She was paddling bow
with Andy Haley, a high school student and friend of the
Scotts. "That huge boat! I knew what I was doing, but at
that point I didn't think I was ready to get killed for any

*Canoe tied up alongside policeboat as the Padma
approaches Pier 8. Alexandra Scott is on deck.*

cause." She shouted to Andy not to get *too* close, but still
she paddled on into the fray.

"The whole thing of death, the possibility of it, was
part of it," Sally Willoughby recalls. The Coast Guard
launches tried to cut her off, but she and Wayne paddled
furiously. "I was scared, but I did see myself as trying to
get in front of the ship. It was a feeling of putting my
body in the way. I'm an awful stubborn person, and I

was really determined to stop that ship. As I look back on it, I sometimes question how far I was actually prepared to go. But I think I was really willing to die."

Wayne Lauser felt good. As he saw the other small boats splash ahead, he felt a unity in the group and knew that, like him, they had made their choice. "As a Quaker, I believe that knowing the truth isn't enough. With knowledge comes a spiritual imperative to act. For me, getting between the ship and the pier was a spiritual process—to go as the Spirit leads."

I also felt a deep calm. In many past actions I had felt the presence of Christ's Spirit. It was almost as if I was going to join God, who was already there, resisting the injustice I had finally seen. Now I felt the familiar touch. I experienced a kind of shimmering peace and energy in the midst of all the splashing confusion and criss-crossed wakes.

A policeman's voice shouted, "O.K., arrest 'em!"

My practical concern was how to get past the Coast Guard launch that had cut across my canoe's path. I could see the steersman only a few yards away, one hand on the wheel, the other on the forward-reverse lever. When my bowman, Chuck Goodwin, and I would paddle hard to the left, the lever would go forward and the cutter would surge ahead a couple of yards. When we'd cut to the right, the lever would come back and the thirty-footer would reverse into our path. Finally, we were almost bumping the larger boat and the sailors' grappling hooks pulled us alongside.

There was nothing to do but get on board, where a city policeman placed us under arrest. As he escorted us firmly into the low-roofed front cabin, we watched the *Padma*, now towering above us, slip into Pier 8. In the hot and crowded cabin, we were surprised and consoled by the young Coast Guard steersman who suddenly leaned over and whispered: "We have to do this job, but we're with you 100 percent. You're doing the right thing."

Patrolman Walter F. Roberts has a friendly, open
face, with hazel eyes and close-cropped blond hair. A
tall, powerfully-built, twenty-two-year-old member of
the police tactical squad, he had already handled over
seventy protest demonstrations—antiwar, black activist, etc. The twin-screwed Coast Guard launches were
highly maneuverable, and it was relatively easy to
swing alongside the demonstrators' little boats as Captain Hayes, from the *Intrepid's* deck, pointed out to the
patrolmen which boats to apprehend.

"That fellow with the daughter told me more about
the *Padma* than I'd ever heard," officer Roberts recalls.
"When we got them aboard, he asked me, 'Do you know
how many people will die as a result of that ship coming
in?' There were tears in his eyes. He was very frustrated. Most people I've arrested in situations like that
have been violent. I've had my share of ducking bottles
and being called all kinds of names. But they were very
polite. Peaceful. There was no profanity. It was probably
the most peaceful demonstration I've seen as a police
officer.

"When I first heard of the demonstration, I dis-
counted it as foolishness. But the thing that amazed me
was their going out in those little boats. We couldn't
believe it. To see a kayak in front of one of those freighters! I was nervous being out there, being that close to
the ship, even in a Coast Guard cutter. I was—I won't
say envious—awed that people would risk their lives like
that. I felt very awkward bringing them in. I was arresting people for doing something they believed in. There
comes a time when you have to make sure order is restored. Sometimes you have to take people into custody
for their own protection. But it wasn't one of my most
rewarding days as a police officer."

Walt Roberts had heard lots of conjecture about the
Padma and had read a little about Pakistan in the Baltimore papers. He never actually approved of this
country's sending arms overseas. He felt uneasy when

Mal Scott said, "Does this make you feel good, bringing all those arms into the port?"

"I said, 'I don't know the situation; we're just trying to protect you.' He kept telling me all kinds of things I didn't know and all I could say was, 'How do you know for sure?' It got me so interested that afterwards I would read articles on Pakistan instead of passing 'em by. I even got a hold of the *New York Times* to find out more.

"When I thought about the demonstration later in the evening, I felt quite sympathetic. This is the only thing you can do to get people to sit up and look. Nobody knew about the situation because it wasn't publicized. The demonstration brought it to public attention. And people didn't like what they read about our government's role.

"Being peaceful, it accomplished more. If it'd been violent, the violence would have got all the attention. In Vietnam demonstrations, people were urging non-violence in Vietnam, but when they're violent here at home, the newspaper reports talk about the violence. Only at the end they say, 'They were against the war.' The message gets completely lost. The public thinks, 'These people are advocating peace, but they're throwing bombs.' The peacefulness of the *Padma* demonstration drove the point home."

By 8:15 P.M., Mal and Alexandra Scott, Wayne Lauser, Sally Willoughby, Stephanie Hollyman, Chuck Goodwin, and I were all aboard Coast Guard cutters or police boats. The other canoes and kayaks stayed clear of the channel and were not picked up. Those in Alex Cox's canoe even had a boatside interview with reporters from the Ladybug's yacht.

Dr. Greenough rushed down late from Johns Hopkins, where he had to see patients. He paddled out in a borrowed yellow foldboat. In the fading light, the police didn't see him, and he slipped inside the cordon, next to the docks. Easing in beside the freighter, he called up to the *Padma*'s crew: "Why are you doing this to East Pakistan?"

*Patrolman Roberts keeps an eye
on the demonstrators he has arrested, as the Padma
slides by to its mooring.*

Hanging over the rail, some of them shouted in response, "Look what you're doing in Vietnam."

"I'm opposed to that too," the doctor called back.

Police churned over to him and pulled him into a cutter. He insisted that they had given him no warning and had no reason to arrest him. They agreed and put him back in the water, saying that if he stayed out longer, they'd arrest him for not having lights on the kayak. Since the ship was docked and nothing more could be done, he paddled back to shore.

"When we got to the dock," Alexandra Scott recalls, "I was put in a station wagon with two police. They started lecturing me about being too young, just doing what my father told me to do. I got really mad. I told them, 'I believe in what I'm doing and I understand it.'

"They said, 'Your father's insane to have his kids out here.'

"I was extremely angry and told them so. 'Being a policeman is just as dangerous,' I said. They kept treating me like a kid, but I think they were surprised at how aware I was and they realized I might have been sincere."

Apparently Sally Willoughby's talks with the arresting officers also had an impact. Some police doing the booking at the station house said, "Why don't you go to Russia?" A policeman who had been on the water rebuked him and then apologized to Sally. "Cops make me uptight," Sally says, "but I try to treat them like human beings. I think they sort of liked us."

In jail the men shared uncomfortable, narrow wooden bunks. The women were put in an ancient detention center, built before the Civil War, that was closed down permanently later that summer. Sally wrote about it later as "an eerie, scary place." The cage-like cells were four and a half feet wide by nine feet long by seven feet high. The narrow bunks had no mattresses. An overhead light stayed on all night. There were no toilet facilities or sinks. Inmates could go to the bathroom only if the matron, a cold, hard woman, deigned to unlock the cell door. Many of the other women were coming down off drugs or alcohol and had no control over their bodies. The cages stank rawly of urine, feces, and vomit. All night there were the sounds of women crying, throwing up, banging on the bars, screaming for a lawyer or calling to go to the bathroom.

"Prison has always been described as a horror story," Sally wrote, "but always in the past it was fiction. It wasn't until I had spent some time in one that I began to feel the reality."

On the morning of July 15, Richard J. Guth, senior prosecutor and assistant State's attorney, arrived at the Southern District Municipal Court at 8:30 A.M. He had heard about the attempted blockade on the 11 o'clock news the night before. The demonstrators were charged with disorderly conduct and the unusual offense of "unlawfully casting loose, setting adrift or placing an object, to wit: a canoe, by obstructing navigation of the S.S. *Padma*." Although he had not gotten much information on the demonstrators, he was aware of sympathetic feelings on the part of people who were following their actions in the mass media.

"Very frankly, I also sympathized with the group," he reminisces. "I had done some reading about what was going on in Pakistan. The group seemed to have a good cause. It seemed a peaceful demonstration. It was a unique thing to do, and I thought it was quite effective. The prosecutor is duty-bound to exercise his discretion in such a way as not to prosecute cases where conviction is not in the public interest or in the interest of justice. I made the judgment not to press for a harsh sentence."

Mr. Guth met briefly with Beatrice Cowan, a Baltimore attorney who agreed on the spur of the moment to represent the demonstrators. He said that the state had no desire to prosecute and would agree to a minimal sentence of "probation without verdict." This did not even involve a guilty finding and would simply place the defendants on thirty days unsupervised probation.

Judge Edgar P. Silver, a short, bald, Jewish man with heavy-rimmed glasses, arrived at the court shortly after State's Attorney Guth. Because of the publicity, he was well aware of the "obstructing navigation" case he would hear.

When the defendants were brought into court, Judge Silver took his seat in the high-backed leather chair between the American and State of Maryland flags. He allowed the demonstrators to make statements explaining their actions, and he was impressed by their motivation and demeanor.

"Privately, I admired people willing to go out in a canoe and shake their fists at a huge ship. It sort of created a David and Goliath atmosphere. I admire anyone who fights for a peaceful cause in a peaceful manner. I admire gentle people and I think these were gentle people. I could tell the police were sympathetic also. The group had a manner about them that seemed to turn even the toughest policeman around."

Judge Silver noted that the prosecutor, in his remarks, laid a foundation somewhat sympathetic to the demonstrators' cause. When Guth suggested a "probation without verdict" sentence, the judge readily agreed.

Upon our release, we joined the rest of the group, picked up our impounded boats at the Marine Police dock, and paddled back out from Broenning Park for a "water picket" of the moored *Padma*. Five police cars and a paddy wagon awaited us at the park when we returned two hours later, but there were no arrests and no problems. I was interviewed at Baltimore's Channel 2 TV station, then, in the afternoon, three of us bought a watermelon and dropped by the Marine Police to share it with the arresting officers. We wanted to continue to have contact with them and we were curious to see what they thought of the action. Talking and spitting seeds, we laughed when officer Roberts said, "You know, this was the first full-scale naval engagement for the Baltimore Police."

At meetings over the next couple of days, we reviewed our accomplishments. We had not stopped the *Padma*, but we had started a movement. We felt sure it would now be possible to do blockades in harbors like Philadelphia, New York, and Boston. More importantly, we had turned a spotlight on an injustice and had created a platform from which to talk to the American people about U.S. support for the Pakistani dictatorship. TV coverage of the blockade had been excellent. A Reuters reporter told us, "This demonstration is going to hit the papers between here and Singapore."

If we could keep up the pace, more and more people would get moving. Editorials would be written. People would begin to write their government representatives, demanding a change in U.S. policy. Sympathetic congresspeople would be supported and apathetic ones would be jogged.

On the day after the *Padma* action, we found that the House Foreign Affairs Committee voted to support a bill to withhold all military and economic aid from Pakistan until the refugees could return safely. We were excited to hear from both congressional aides and Bangladesh Information Center people that our action was instrumental in the positive vote. Tom Dine, of Senator Church's staff, said the action especially fortified the infrastructure of congressional staff people who were working on the Pakistan issue night and day. It also helped support legislators who needed more impetus to take on the Executive Branch.

"Any time you get people willing to blockade a boat," he said later, "it means that the government's policy either hasn't been explained or can't be."

Jack Patterson found that there was a many-fold increase in the Baltimore area of people attentive to the Bangladesh issue and willing to work on it. After the action, Dr. Greenough was able to see Senator Kennedy personally, and soon afterwards the senator made a personal trip to Bengali refugee camps in India.

Finally, there was the personal dimension. The action had been fun and exciting, satisfying and spiritually moving. For Alex Cox it was like living for awhile the way people are meant to live—helping each other out, sharing decision-making, using your talents in a good cause, feeling that you're where you ought to be instead of just feeling badly you're not part of the action. For Jack Patterson it had been—excepting civil rights demonstrations—probably "the most coherent, intense, and graphic experience of nonviolence I've ever been a part of."

Alexandra Scott reminisced later: "It was a great feeling—all these people fighting against those big guys we never see."

*Overloaded with desperate Bengali refugees,
an Indian bus passes the abandoned
corpse of an infant killed by cholera.*

CHAPTER 5

The Longshoremen Get Involved

"I.L.A. Means 'I Love America.' " The huge red, white, and blue banner across the lobby of Miami's DiLido Hotel only increased our anxiety about coming to the national convention of the 110,000-member International Longshoremen's Association. The convention sessions, we soon discovered, began with several hundred ILA members singing "The Star Spangled Banner" and the Canadian National Anthem, reciting the Pledge of Allegiance to the Flag, and listening attentively to a patriotic sermon by a local clergyman.

"This is an impossible situation," Sultana thought. How could we ever communicate to these staunch patriots about the government's role in oppression and atrocity? How could four university-educated types, who'd never hefted a cargo hook or driven a fork-lift, convince calloused dock workers not to load Pakistani ships, especially when it would mean losing thousands of dollars in pay?

In Baltimore, Sultana, Anna Taylor, and others had met with the local dock workers and urged them not to handle the *Padma*'s cargo. Perhaps it was our picketing, the publicity, and the appeal of two lovely women with foreign accents, for the union shunned the boat for two days. On July 16, however, threatened by a lawsuit and assured by the shipper that no military cargo was to be put on board, the workers loaded the ship.

But what if we could get the ILA nationally to boycott Pakistani cargoes, we asked ourselves? After all, John Resta of the Philadelphia ILA had invited Sultana and me to the convention. So, while the Baltimore ILA was loading the *Padma*, four of us were winging our way to Miami Beach, with little eels of nervousness swimming in our guts.

Though our Miami team was put together hurriedly, the choice of members was not without forethought. Sultana would bring her poise, intellectual sharpness, and persuasiveness. Monayem Chowdhury was a knowledgeable and committed male Bengali. A short, soft-spoken, Gandhi-like man of thirty-six, his mother and brother still lived in East Bengal. Many U.S.-based Bengalis were afraid of repercussions on relatives at home and were understandably reluctant to identify themselves openly with the Bangladesh cause. But Monayem broke off his Ph.D. studies in economics, became vice-president of Friends of East Bengal, and spent most of his savings and assets in the struggle. "The injustice was so strong, I had to accept the risks."

Sultana described our third team member, Jim Bristol, as "venerable-looking." White-haired, slow-speaking, meticulous, going on sixty, Jim was known in Quaker circles for his deep commitment to nonviolence. He and his wife had been directors of the Quaker Center in New Delhi in the late fifties, during which time they arranged Coretta and Martin Luther King's visit to observe the Gandhian movement.

"When you called, I was at the American Friends Service Committee," Jim recalls, "working like a horse with blinders on the repeal of the military draft. But I saw I could get away on Friday and join you for the weekend. I've been concerned about the whole Indian subcontinent for years. I was glad to be able to do something."

Our Friday evening arrival at first seemed our undoing. The desk clerk informed us that we were between two conventions, the international and the national. Many delegates, including ILA President "Teddy" Gleason, were away on a cruise.

"There won't be any sessions until Monday," he said. To cap it off, John Resta, who had invited us, was home sick in Philadelphia.

We were downcast. On the off chance that Richard Askew, president of Philadelphia's ILA, had not joined the cruise, I got his room number at the desk and called. He was in. I explained briefly our concern and mentioned John Resta's invitation.

The strong, resonant voice on the other end of the line said, "Come on up tomorrow and we'll talk."

Richard Askew made an immediate impression. "We stepped into his hotel room and I looked up at this enormous, powerful black man against the sun of the window," Sultana remembers. "As soon as he talked, he overwhelmed me with a sense of dignity and integrity. But I was frightened. Here we were, walking in absolutely cold off the street. He was our only contact. How did we know where he stands in the organization? How did we know he'd put us in touch with the right people?"

I mentioned something about Jim's and my concern for East Bengal coming from our Quaker background. Mr. Askew smiled and turned to the other three union men in the room: "The Quakers," he said. "Always stirring up trouble." But then he went on with a little lecture about how Quakers, long before the civil rights movement, had helped free the slaves. He said he served on the board of the YMCA with a Quaker lawyer—"a really fine man."

When Mr. Chowdhury was introduced, Mr. Askew noted that he taught economics at Lincoln University, one of the top black colleges on the East Coast. He commented on the excellence of Sultana's English ("How come a Bengali lady speaks with such a perfect accent?") and watched her with raised eyebrows as she told her story of East Bengal.

She spoke of the budding democracy, the free elections, and the way the dictatorship crushed the people's aspirations. She spoke of genocide, the attempt to wipe out a race, a culture, a people—a pogrom. She gave documented evidence of the soldiers' savagery. She talked about the economic exploitation of the East by the West. Gently but firmly (I held my breath) she told how the U.S. government had allied itself with Yahya Khan.

"Americans have a special responsibility," she said. "American money is helping the regime to survive. As Bengalis we have no rights in this country. What happens to us and our people depends entirely on people like you."

Mr. Askew responded with unconcealed fervor. "It sounds like the situation of black people and other colored people in this country and the rest of the world. A small group is trying to suppress the majority. I'm for the downtrodden. I'll introduce you to some other people and I'll do my best to get you on the convention floor."

At 8 P.M., we met again in the same room, this time with six union men, including John Bowers, the international union's executive vice-president. Sultana and Monayem spoke again. Although some of the men were confused ("Yahya Khan? You mean that rich playboy, Aly Khan?"), strong sympathy was expressed for the Bengali cause.

We talked tactics. Given the sympathy, what could the ILA do? Bowers was very direct. "I'm with you. I don't want the union to load *any* arms for Pakistan. In fact, I wish we wouldn't load ships for the U.S.S.R. or the other Communist countries either." Bowers said he had backed the boycott of the *Padma* and had only supported loading it when assured no military goods were to be put aboard. He mentioned in passing that George Meany was sympathetic to not loading arms.

"I'm going to meet Gleason and Meany Monday morning," Bowers said. "I hope we can get you onto the convention floor. I hope we'll pass a resolution not to load any arms for Pakistan."

Suddenly our hopes were soaring. Bowers seemed an absolutely key contact. But what about a broader resolution not to load *any* material on Pakistani ships? Doesn't economic aid prop up the dictatorship as much as military, we argued? Bowers didn't know. He didn't think the union would go that far. But Askew said quietly and firmly: "We won't load *anything* on Pakistani ships in Philadelphia, no matter what."

There seemed to be nothing to do on Sunday, so we slept late, then hired a small motor boat and buzzed through the canals past the skyscraper hotels of Miami Beach. We bought soup and sandwich material at a local grocery and ate in our rooms.

But Richard Askew had been pleading our cause, and Monday morning, July 19, found us in the DiLido coffee shop's cafeteria line, getting breakfast courtesy of "the boss," Teddy Gleason.

He struck Sultana as a raw sort of person, really off the docks, a short man, dressed with everything in bad taste. But he was business-like, obviously knowledgeable, and not unfriendly. "I know your problem and we're not gonna load any arms," he stated flatly.

We tried to raise the question of economic aid supporting the regime's atrocities. Reports showed that aid was not getting through to help the suffering people. UNICEF jeeps, for example, had been spotted being used by Pakistani troops on patrol. Also, given the ease with which shippers can falsify manifests (in Canada, they called F-86 Sabre-jet parts "foodstuffs and cancer-treatment equipment"), might not military supplies slip through the docks disguised as humanitarian aid?

"If we want to know what's in the crates, we can find out," he claimed. "We checked the *Padma*. It just had food."

I gave him a copy of the July 15 *Baltimore Sun*, with the State Department release describing the military equipment on the *Padma*. He read it quickly and picked out one item. "Twenty-two calibre ammunition isn't significant," he said.

"They're killing people with it," Sultana replied tightly.

"We'd make fools of ourselves if we didn't load food and medicine," he shot back. "Congress hasn't cut off economic aid, why should we? We're not a political body."

Richard Askew, who'd held his peace up to this point, spoke slowly: "All the aid is going to help fifty million people oppress seventy million. They're acting like Hitler. We shouldn't work *any* ships going to Pakistan. It'll all just go to help the military."

Gleason was adamant, but then softened a bit. "We can't get in the position of not sending food and medicines. But you have a point if the aid's not really getting through to the people who need it. I'll check with Meany about economic aid."

With Gleason's O.K., we set up a literature table just outside the ballroom where convention sessions were held. We handed out dozens of leaflets and found delegates generally sympathetic. The ILA group from India gave us a warm welcome and promised enthusiastic support. The All-India Dock Workers Association sent a telegram to the convention, congratulating the Baltimore ILA for not loading arms and saying that this will save thousands of lives.

Monayem, a Moslem, talked for an hour with the Turkish delegation. He and I also met with Harry Bridges, the radical president of the West Coast Longshoremen's Association, and got a strong statement of support.

Remembering John Bowers' statement about George Meany's interest, I called the labor chief's hotel room, expecting to get through to a secretary or an aide. But Meany himself answered, and I found myself nervously explaining our Miami mission to the world's most powerful labor leader. He was sympathetic and said he hoped the ILA wouldn't handle any cargoes. He made clear, though, that he wouldn't try to influence them. "The ILA itself has to decide," he said.

I noted from the convention agenda that Bayard Rustin would speak to the Wednesday session. I had known Bayard slightly from civil rights work in the sixties, when he was a close associate of Martin Luther King. Luckily, I had his private home phone number. I called him in New York and arranged to meet him upon his arrival. He agreed that the boycott should be total and said he would both talk to Gleason and state his views in his convention speech.

"A big problem," he noted, "is that ILA unemployment is 15 percent. Not loading ships will mean fewer jobs for the men."

Even with all the progress so far, we were still anxious about the outcome. We couldn't help but ask ourselves if we were just being babied along. We wondered how seriously they were taking us, given their full convention agenda, with speeches by Senators Hubert Humphrey and Henry Jackson and other dignitaries. They were bound to be concerned mostly about their expiring three-year contract with the shipping industry and the prospect of a long, crippling strike. Could they really think about a small country eight thousand miles away?

Rank-and-file people going in and out of the ballroom kept saying, "Get to Teddy. He's the boss." We had seen Gleason, but he had said nothing definite about our speaking to the convention. So far everything was at the level of fuzzy verbal commitment. We kept checking with Mr. Askew, who assured us several times a day that everything was going all right.

That night John Chancellor on the NBC evening news quoted the Indian foreign minister as stating that $35 million of military aid is still in the pipeline to Pakistan and that this may harm U.S.-India relations. Chancellor mentioned that a Pakistani ship left Baltimore last week, carrying military goods which critics said would be used by the Pakistan army against the people of East Pakistan.

Tuesday morning's session was crammed with

speeches by political figures, including Senator Humphrey and Texas State Senator Barbara Jordan, a dynamic black woman who later won a seat in the U.S. House. As the afternoon meeting began, Sultana was suddenly ushered to the platform and told that she had three minutes to state the Bengali case.

"I realized I couldn't go into any detail, so I gave a simple analysis of the economic exploitation of East Pakistan. I told how Bengalis had tried democratic political processes and had these taken away by one subterfuge or another. In appealing to the ILA not to load ships, I said, 'They're human beings whose lives are at stake. It's within your power to decide if they have a right to live or die.' "

When Sultana finished, Gleason, who was presiding, said to the convention, "Now we support this and we won't touch arms to Pakistan. We'll also support congressional efforts to end military and economic aid."

We expected a vote or some kind of resolution to follow Gleason's statement, but we soon realized that having "the boss" make this commitment on the convention floor put the ILA on official record.

We would have appreciated a more total ban on loading *all* Pakistan cargoes, but we were elated to have accomplished so much. As we packed our bags, we rejoiced that the commitment not to load arms was now a nationwide ILA policy, not just the Baltimore local's practice. Moreover, we had gotten a powerful international union to support the Bengali cause. It would add enormously to the movement to be able to say that we now have the longshoremen's backing.

We realized that the ILA stand would also increase pressure on Congress and the Administration to change the policy of supporting Yahya Khan. The experience that we had in Miami helped us grow from a small, Philadelphia-based group of nonviolent activists to a group with nationwide outreach and much greater political clout.

The Pakistani freighter Al Ahmadi edges past a pier and toward the canoes of the nonviolent fleet.

CHAPTER 6

Spreading the Blockade

When we returned to Philadelphia, the challenge was to keep the issue before the public and to continue trying to block the aid flow. Our most dramatic and meaningful way of highlighting the situation was through another ship blockade. While the ILA team was in Miami, Bill Moyer had gone to New York City to consult with peace groups and the local chapter of the Bangladesh League of America. Great interest was expressed in the ship-blocking method and, as luck would have it, a Pakistani ship, the *Sutlej*, was expected in the port on July 22.

The attempted blockade aborted when dangerous harbor currents almost swept away two rowboats and a canoe manned by the New York group's hastily assembled "nonviolent fleet." But Bill participated in a picket line in front of the *Sutlej*'s dock and helped organize a memorial service near the *Sutlej* the next day. Over one hundred people participated, carrying signs reading "End U.S. Support of Pakistani Genocide," "Send Medicine, Not Bombers," and "Sutlej: Another Death Ship." The Saturday edition of the *New York Post* carried a good picture-article on the demonstration, and it was also covered by CBS network TV.

While in New York, Bill was contacted by a group of Boston peace activists wanting to know how they could help. Bill suggested a number of strategies including ship-blocking. Although few Pakistani ships come to Boston, the group organized a small nonviolent fleet and, later in the summer, threatened to use it against an in-coming Pakistani freighter. The ship turned and never entered the port.

We could not rely solely on ship-blocking, however. Pakistani ships didn't dock every day and information on those that did enter the port was still hard to obtain. This was again made clear when Fran Woods, our chief port information person, visited the Philadelphia Maritime Exchange, which normally puts listings of in-coming ships on a big board in their office. She explained that she was a Catholic sister and might like to send relief aid to refugees in East Pakistan. How could she find out about Pakistani ships?

"Let me tell you what's been happening," the person at the desk confided. "A group has been picketing Pakistani ships. They even tried to block one with their own boats. We've been instructed not to make public any information on ships to Pakistan. We're not supposed to put them on the big board or to list them in the *Journal of Commerce*."

The man hinted that police and the Coast Guard were also "in on it." And indeed, when Fran called the Coast Guard, she was told that they couldn't give out any definite information.

Given this uncertainty, the Direct Action Committee began to plan for two possible scenarios. One involved getting ready for a blockade of the three Pakistani ships—the *Al Ahmadi*, the *Al Hasan*, and the *Rangmati*—still listed in the *Journal of Commerce* as coming to Philadelphia, possibly as soon as the coming week. The other assumed no Pakistani ships until August and focused on a series of marches, picket lines, and other actions both to keep a sense of momentum and to build drama and public interest toward the eventual arrival of the ship.

We called a large organizing meeting on Sunday, July

25, at a downtown Friends meetinghouse. Interest was strong. About one hundred people attended. Not only had they heard about the *Padma* blockade, but the July 23 papers carried State Department field reports, released by Sen. Edward Kennedy, predicting "famine conditions, involving widespread hunger, suffering and perhaps starvation" for East Pakistan in the coming year. The July 24 *New York Times* said that senior government officials, at the prodding of Senator Symington, admitted that about fifteen million dollars worth of U.S. arms was in the process of being shipped to Pakistan. People were becoming more aware of our government's culpability in breaking the fabric of life in East Pakistan.

General approval was expressed for the two scenarios. Small groups or individuals took responsibility for laying the groundwork—ship research, demonstrator recruitment, ILA contacts, leaflets, press contacts, fundraising, police liaison, sign-making, legal research, canoe-gathering, and overall coordination.

On Monday, July 26, I checked in with Richard Askew and found him as determined as ever not to load any Pakistani ships, military cargo or not. He said he would let us know of any Pakistani ship arrivals and that the Philadelphia ILA would not load any ship where we erected a picket line.

In the meantime, Bill was talking with Mr. Chris Donohue, manager of the local office of the London-based firm Furness-Withy, the company handling Pakistani ships in Philadelphia. When Bill explained our purpose and asked that Furness-Withy not handle Pakistani ships, he got a tongue-lashing.

"I will put an injunction on you if you picket the pier," Mr. Donohue snapped over the phone. "It costs thousands of dollars to load a ship. I don't intend to lose money on this. Your action may well cause violence on the piers. People who've tried to block longshoremen have been known to be found in the river."

Bill said that we would be nonviolent, but if there were violence, it would be minor compared to what's happening in East Pakistan. He said that we would like to settle the matter by negotiation, but, if Furness-Withy's office was adamant, we would picket it as well as the pier.

Later in the day, Lt. George Fencl, of the police Civil Disobedience Squad (a Philadelphia unit specially designed to handle demonstrations) confirmed Fran Woods's information that police were "in on" the maneuverings about ship information. Fencl called Charles Walker and said that he had talked with Donohue and that the *Al Ahmadi* visit was now cancelled and the *Al Hasan* might by-pass Philadelphia.

We had negotiated before with Lieutenant Fencl in anti-Vietnam war and civil rights demonstrations. We knew that he was sometimes a helpful, even sympathetic, police officer who respected the right to demonstrate. This time, however, he seemed to be trying to throw us off the track by suggesting that no more freighters would be coming and our blockade plans were therefore meaningless.

On Tuesday, July 27, fifty of us began picketing the downtown offices of Furness-Withy at Sixth and Chestnut Streets, near historic Independence Hall. Our leaflet called for an end to all U.S. trade and aid to Pakistan until the killing was stopped and democracy restored. It urged a massive international effort to aid the victims of the Pakistani army. Street speakers from the group made the point that the problem would be resolved if Furness-Withy, and similar shippers elsewhere, would recognize their moral responsibility and not handle Pakistani ships. Signs said: "A Half-Million Killed, Eight Million Refugees," "Ships Loading in Phila. Help Kill Bengalis," "Would 'Aid' to Hitler Have Helped the Jews?"

A delegation to Mr. Donohue was received more graciously than Bill had been on the phone. He apologized for his veiled threat, said that he was sympathetic to our cause, but that if he didn't handle the ship, another company would.

"I'm just an agent," he argued. "Business is slow and we need the business."

We sympathized with his problem, but questioned the stance of putting business ahead of human life. On the question of other shippers handling the cargoes, we asked Mr. Donohue to contact the other companies and urge all of them not to handle Pakistani ships.

"That's not realistic," he said.

As Cesar Chavez and others have proved, day-in-day-out picketing can be a solid method of direct action and we were glad to use it. We scheduled a picket at Furness-Withy every day from 12 noon to 1:30 P.M. This schedule gave sympathizers a chance to come demonstrate over a long lunch hour, but not get burnt out by a long-duration action.

But there must be dozens, if not hundreds, of picket lines in the United States on any one day—Farm Worker support groups at supermarkets, striking workers in front of factories, etc. Only a few of these can be covered by the mass media. In order to continue to reach and educate the public with our message, we knew we needed more than a picket line.

Through his years of work with the civil rights movement, Billy Moyer had been developing a concept of nonviolent direct action called "sociodrama."

"What you're trying to do in nonviolence," he would say in our meetings, "is to paint a clear picture of an injustice that violates widely accepted values of the American people. When the black students at Greensboro, North Carolina, sat down at lunch counters, asked for a hamburger, and got beat up and jailed, you didn't have to do much explaining. The news and TV photos told the whole story. It was high drama and it educated most Americans."

Invariably at this point someone would say, "But

nonviolence shouldn't be just media-oriented. I don't think we should design all our actions just to get on the six o'clock TV news."

"I agree," Bill would answer. "Nonviolence is a lot more than reaching the mass media. It's noncooperation with an injustice, working against it, looking for the truth, meeting the opposition with goodwill, and showing that there's a better alternative."

"Then why the big media focus?"

"Because," Bill would explain, "we're convinced that the government's policy is wrong and we want to convince others. We'll never change the policy with just ourselves. We've got to reach thousands, maybe millions of people. We have to do public education. I can talk every night for one hundred years to audiences of one hundred people, and still not reach nearly as many people as if I get on the CBS evening news just one time. I can pass out hundreds of thousands of leaflets and still not reach anything like the audience Walter Cronkite reaches every night."

With this in mind, we began to build on the basic format of picketing, street-speaking, negotiations with Mr. Donohue, and harbor actions.

At one point, we took advantage of Furness-Withy's location near Independence Hall. First securing a permit from the U.S. Park Police, we set up an "East Pakistan Voting Booth" directly in front of Independence Hall. Four demonstrators, dressed in typical Bengali *saris* and *lungis,* approached a table, cast their "ballot," and then smilingly shook hands with other demonstrators whose signs and costumes identified them as members of the Awami League.

While this was happening, a more ominous group was forming a block away. Five "sailors" carried large cardboard replicas of Pakistani ships from Furness-Withy toward the voting scene. "On board" were four "West Pakistani soldiers," dressed in black shirts and military hats and carrying realistic looking toy guns. When they arrived, the soldiers "opened fire" on the voters. Many visitors to the Liberty Bell probably were not aware of this different kind of freedom message until the guns started rattling and they saw screaming, ketchup-soaked Bengali voters sprawling across the pavement.

The drama was interpreted by a demonstrator with a bullhorn and by others handing out leaflets. A local TV crew made us run through the scene twice to make sure they caught the details. The evening news featured the sociodrama and an up-date on the situation in Pakistan.

On Thursday, July 29, the nonviolent fleet was launched into the Port of Philadelphia "for maneuvers." Six canoes, two kayaks, two rowboats, and two out-boards crept down the Delaware River from a public park on the New Jersey side, under the awesome span of the Benjamin Franklin Bridge, and over to Pier 48, where we understood Pakistani ships normally docked.

One of the outboards joined us when we were well out on the river. We were surprised to learn that it was piloted by a young New Jersey policeman who had a few days vacation and said he wanted to support us. We were also caught off guard when invited aboard the tugboat *Triton*, whose crew was obviously overcome with curiosity. We thought the cocky tugboaters might be hostile to our trespassing on their turf, but they were friendly and seemed to understand our concern. They warned us about the danger of being flipped by big ships and tugs, but fed us a delicious three-course lunch, prepared by their Chinese cook. We climbed back over the *Triton*'s big side bumpers and dropped into our canoes, then paddled around the pier area, seeking the best line-up to block a ship.

All three local TV channels covered the "maneuvers." The *Philadelphia Evening Bulletin*, the city's biggest evening paper, carried a good article and photo. The *Camden Courier Post*, the largest nearby New Jersey paper, did a full-page article with three excellent photos of the fleet.

On Friday, July 30, ten of us picketed Furness-Withy in the rain. Our spirits were lifted when someone brought us a copy of the early edition of the *Evening Bulletin* with a long, illustrated article "Canoeists Trying to Help Bengalis," by the popular columnist Rose DeWolf.

"Can a dozen or so canoes blockade the Port of Philadelphia and prevent a huge ocean freighter from docking here?" Rose's article asked. She went on to give an excellent rundown of the situation in Pakistan, including the U.S. role in supplying arms and money. "We often think of foreign policy," she concluded, "as something strictly conceived and carried out in Washington, as something we ordinary citizens do not decide. But a group of Philadelphians who plan to paddle out in mosquito-sized boats to swarm around an elephant-sized freighter obviously don't believe that. 'Foreign policy' is happening here."

The week of August 1 brought major publicity and legislative breakthroughs at the national level. On Sunday, George Harrison and Ringo Starr, of Beatles fame, joined Ravi Shankar, Bob Dylan, and other entertainers for a Madison Square Garden benefit that raised $250,000 for the refugees. Ex-Senator Eugene McCarthy hit the press when he called for recognition of Bangladesh. The *New York Times* urged editorially that all aid to Yahya Khan's regime be unequivocally stopped. Aid puts the U.S. in a position of "subsidizing crimes against humanity unequaled since Hitler's time," the *Times* said.

The August 2 issues of both *Time* and *Newsweek* carried front page stories—"Pakistan's Agony" and "Bengal: The Murder of a People"—detailing the situation and carrying incredible photos of the suffering, exhausted, starving Bengali refugees. The *Newsweek* story began with a particularly horrifying report of a West Pakistani major asking young men in a Bengali village to be blood donors for wounded soldiers. When

they agreed and lay down on makeshift cots, needles
were inserted in their veins and their blood was drained
out until they died.

Fourteen Pakistani diplomats—all of Bengali origin
—quit government posts at the Pakistani embassy or
United Nations mission, charging Khan's government
with crimes against humanity. In Washington, the
House of Representatives, passing a $3.4-billion foreign
aid authorization bill, went on record as opposing further aid to Pakistan.

In response, President Nixon finally bestirred himself
to make one of his few statements on the situation.
Rather than speaking out against the atrocities, he took
the occasion of an August 5 news conference to defend
his policy. He rejected rising congressional and public
pressure, saying that continued aid is a way for the U.S.
to "influence the course of events." And aid cut-off, he
argued, would be "totally counterproductive" and
would aggravate the refugees' problems.

We continued the noontime picketing, street speaking, and negotiation at Furness-Withy throughout the
week. On Friday, we tried an innovation that attracted
renewed press interest. We contacted Bob Dickenson,
an architect and artist active in the peace movement,
and asked him to design a lightweight, portable mural
depicting the impact of U.S. aid. Bob put together a
cleverly-constructed featherboard panel, five feet high
and forty feet long, which could easily be dismantled
into five-by-five sections. At one end of the panel, he
drew a picture of U.S. ships being loaded with arms and
other aid. At the other end, he sketched Bengali refugee
families living in sewer pipes—a scene inspired by a
dramatic *Time* magazine photo depicting refugees in
Calcutta using sewer pipes as their only shelter. When
assembled, the panel dramatically showed the correla-
tion between U.S. aid and Bengali suffering.

At Friday's picket, we erected the panel and had demonstrators paint in the colors to finish the mural. Later,

*Dick Taylor does street speaking in front of
the portable mural elected in downtown Philadelphia.*

we would carry the dismantled mural on marches and
then erect it at a demonstration site. Channel 10 TV
carried the mural-building on its news show.

On Sunday, August 8, over one hundred demonstrators, some in the water with a nonviolent fleet of canoes,
a sailboat, and a rowboat, picketed Pier 48. Calls to radio
and TV stations, newspapers, and the wire services on
August 7 showed the variety and unpredictability of the
press. Some showed little interest in the demonstration,
while other reporters took extensive notes or made tape
recordings of what we had to say. A correspondent for
WCAU radio said that a friend was just back from Pakistan and that she was so interested in the story that she
would cover it on her own time.

The *Philadelphia Inquirer* carried a front-page photo
story on the demonstration, quoted Bill Moyer, and edi-
torialized against aid to Pakistan. The *Bulletin* had an
article and supportive editorial and the *Daily News* a

photo story. Channels 6 and 10 also covered the story on both the early and late evening news shows. We were delighted to have blitzed all the major news media in the city.

The reason for the growing focus on the waterfront was that rumors were abounding that a Pakistani freighter, the *Al Ahmadi*, might arrive soon. We were amazed when a man in a business suit, who obviously had a high position at a dockside stevedore company, told Carol Deming, a picketer, that the *Al Ahmadi* was due soon and that she could contact him for further information. Demonstrators from the suburbs started camping out near the Delaware River, several miles south of Philadelphia, using binoculars for reconnaissance of in-coming ships. We found that it took about one-and-a-half hours from the time they spotted a ship until it arrived in the vicinity of Pier 48, just enough warning, since it took about an hour to paddle to the pier from Pyne Point Park, our launch spot in New Jersey. When picketer Vint Deming set up another reconnaissance camp farther south, near Newark, Delaware, with a tent and tripod-mounted telescope, Channel 12 did a story on it for its two evening news shows.

As the excitement grew, we began getting more frequent calls from Lieutenant Fencl of the police Civil Disobedience Squad. He said that he was in contact with Furness-Withy, and that no ship was expected. Carol Deming, however, called her stevedore company contact and was told that the *Al Ahmadi* would arrive on Thursday afternoon, August 12. Mr. Askew at ILA said the boat would come in to Pier 80 at 1 P.M.

On Thursday at 11 A.M., therefore, we launched a nonviolent fleet of seven canoes and one kayak. We paddled to Pier 80 and found it guarded by a Coast Guard cutter, several Philadelphia Marine Police boats, and a state Marine Patrol launch. Eighty demonstrators, including two representatives of the clergy, picketed the pier entrance on the shore. Newspaper and TV reporters and more than a hundred hard-hatted dock workers looked on.

At 1:30, Bill called the picketers and canoes to wharf-side for an important announcement. He asked Father Joe Daust, a Catholic priest, to say a prayer. Then he told the enthusiastic crowd that he had learned from the Bay Pilots that the *Al Ahmadi* had turned tail and left the port. Learning of our blockade and the long-shoremen's determination not to load, the ship had made a U-turn and was heading for Baltimore.

"We've stopped a ship. This is a great victory for our cause," Bill shouted to everyone's cheers.

We met back at Pyne Point Park for a strategy meeting. Bill and I would have called it a day, but enthusiasm was high and the group decided to go to Baltimore to keep the pressure on the *Al Ahmadi*. Before leaving, we switched on the radio and TV news. Channels 3 and 10 were giving the demonstration great coverage and radio stations KYW and WCAU were saying that the ship had been diverted due to the successful blockade. Later newspaper reports confirmed the fact that the blockade was the main reason for the ship's changing course.

Confusion about where the ship was docking pre-vented a successful blocking action in Baltimore, but a "water picket" of three canoes, and a land picket, using Bob Dickenson's mural, were covered by the city's news media. The Baltimore ILA, whose leadership didn't take as strong a stand as the Philadelphia unit, said the ship didn't have a military cargo and loaded it.

Thinking that we might have scared Pakistani ships away from Philadelphia, at least temporarily, we began to lay plans to go to Washington. We had been deeply moved by photos of Bengali refugees living in stacks of unused sewer pipes in Calcutta. We wondered if we might somehow replicate their plight by constructing a "refugee camp" near the White House. While we con-sidered next steps, Bill went to Chicago to help a group there develop an action against World Airways, the air-

Pickets protest outside Philadelphia's Pier 80, while the nonviolent fleet blocks the Al Ahmadi.

line leasing Boeing 707s to Pakistan. They picketed the World Airways office tower, while some demonstrators slipped upstairs and began filling the air with leaflets made into paper airplanes, representing the 707s used by the Pakistani military. Police rushed to stop this, but each time they arrived at a window where demonstrators had been spotted, the demonstrators' heads would disappear and paper airplanes would begin floating down from another window a few floors above or below them.

Later, Dick Murray, who had originally alerted Bill to the Pakistan situation, was arrested in a rowboat while he and a priest dumped "bodies" (made of balloons and dressed in rags, with red dye in the pockets) into the Chicago River. Demonstrators on shore circulated leaflets comparing the balloon bodies with the rotting Bengali corpses floating down the Ganges. Dick and the priest, Father Bill Hogan, were jailed for "depositing unwholesome substances" in the river.

Before we had gotten far into Washington plans, Carol Deming's stevedore company contact reported that the *Al Ahmadi* would make another try at Philadelphia. The Pilots' Association confirmed that it was due early Tuesday morning, August 17. Wanting to make sure that it didn't slip by us with a dawn arrival, we struggled out of bed at 4 A.M. on the seventeenth. By 5:30, four canoes and a kayak were in the water. By seven o'clock, they had covered the three miles to Pier 80, where several police and Coast Guard boats were waiting.

The scene in front of the pier was mass confusion. Our thirty-member picket line was being respected, not only by the longshoremen, but also by a growing line of teamster-driven trucks that were backing up along Delaware Avenue.

A short, muscular, red-faced man, who described himself as an ILA international representative, stormed up to me and yelled that the men were losing money by not loading the ship. A large group of dockworkers, their role on the pier identified by the color of their hard-hats, crowded around while I struggled to interpret Richard Askew's views to a man who must have been well aware of them.

While he kept shouting, "You're taking bread out of their families' mouths!" teamsters were stomping around, demanding to know why they couldn't take their loads to a Japanese ship, tied up at the southern end of the pier. Shipping company representatives were also blustering around, complaining about losing money. Finally, we agreed to picket only the entrance where the *Al Ahmadi* was due, in exchange for a commitment from the stevedore company to steer longshoremen and trucks only to the Japanese ship.

At 10 A.M., our spotters down-river reported sighting

the *Al Ahmadi*. Warehouses jutting into the river blocked all but our straight ahead-view. I walkie-talkied Vint Deming, circling among the police boats in his aluminum canoe, and heard his voice crackle: "I can see it coming up under the Walt Whitman Bridge . . . . Now it's only five piers away."

Vint and the others looked like slivers of dark wood on the glistening water, bouncing two hundred yards away at the riverside entrance to the dock. Suddenly, we saw two canoeists raise their cardboard "Stop the Death Ship" signs above their heads and point them downriver. In a moment, the enormous green and gray prow of the *Al Ahmadi* edged past the warehouse to our right, nudged by two large tugs.

The small flotilla paddled straight for the bow, but the police, apparently with orders not to make arrests, pulled alongside, grabbed them, gunned engines, and dragged the canoes away. As soon as the paddlers were released, however, they stroked right back into the tugboat wakes. We held our breath as our tiny boats cut directly across the huge bow. For a good twenty minutes, the minuet of canoe advance and canoe-police retreat continued, while transfixed longshoremen, teamsters, shore demonstrators, news reporters, TV cameramen, and Pakistani crewmen leaning over the rail watched. Finally, the *Al Ahmadi* was able to snag a hawser on the dock's mooring post.

Somehow I couldn't accept the finality of that hawser. I walked nervously onto the pier and spoke to the dock worker securing it.

"How about giving us a hand and not tying up the ship?" I asked.

"I'm just doing my job," he said in a gruff, but not unfriendly, way.

"Well, would you mind if I untied it?" I asked.

"Suit yourself," he said and stepped back.

I pulled the big rope off the post and threw it as far as I could out onto the water. Immediately there were police

A police launch approaches a canoe
near the Al Ahmadi's bow.

at my elbows and I was escorted off the pier. The dock
workers now grappled for the floating rope, but canoeist
Stephanie Hollyman (a student visiting Philadelphia
from Bennington College) plunged into the foul waters,
grabbed the line, and swam away with it. A police launch
swept in beside her, pulled her unceremoniously by her
belt into the boat, and ferried the hawser to the dock.

Another canoe paddled over to the dock and Steward
Hyman, a student at Pendle Hill, a local Quaker study
center, clambered up the side to try to unhook the line
again. A dock worker shoved him off the pier, but as he
fell, he just managed to grab the line. He dangled there a

moment, twenty feet above the water, then started climbing slowly up toward the ship, while TV cameras whirred and everyone watched in fascination. When he had hand-over-handed about halfway up, the *Al Ahmadi* crew shook him off the line and he fell into the water, where he was also picked up by police.

The longshoremen held the final card. They had watched all this and everything now depended on whether they would load or not. I rushed to Richard Askew's office with a Bengali demonstrator. We urged him to come to the pier and make a statement to the men and the press. It was a little after 11 A.M., and we pointed out that a work gang was scheduled to come through the gates at 1 P.M.

At 12:30 the work crew began arriving. We intensified our picketing. We tried to put a leaflet in every man's hand and to explain what we were doing. At 12:45, Richard Askew arrived, driving a large, black Chrysler into the middle of the crowd. He got out slowly and was immediately besieged with microphones and questions by reporters.

Speaking deliberately, he said: "I'm not here to tell the men what to do. I think they've already decided what to do. I'm here to express my convictions. This company should be ashamed to have this ship tied up at its dock. West Pakistan is committing genocide on East Pakistan. If we load this ship, it would be like helping to commit genocide."

A reporter asked the question that had been thrown at demonstrators all morning: "Mr. Askew, aren't your men losing money by not loading this ship?"

Without the slightest hesitation, he replied: "If I know in my heart that the money I'm earning is blood money, then I don't want to have anything to do with it." With that, he piled back into his car and drove off. When he left, the whole work crew vanished with him.

A longshoreman tipped us off to the phone number used by the shipping company to recruit men for jobs, and through the rest of the day and night we phoned in and heard their regular pleas for *Al Ahmadi* workers. Not a single longshoreman crossed our picket line, which we organized on a continuous day-and-night basis. Fewer and fewer workers even showed up at the gates and, the next afternoon, the *Al Ahmadi* sailed away, leaving 1,135 tons of equipment on the dock.

It seems clear that this action completely shut the port of Philadelphia to Pakistani ships. Two weeks after the *Al Ahmadi* left, a local attorney phoned me saying he represented a manufacturer who wanted to ship tallow to Pakistan. The *Al Ahmadi* was in Baltimore, he said, but would like to return to Philadelphia. Would we permit them to load an innocuous product like tallow? "I'm pleading for tallow manufacturers and soap factories," he urged in his best Philadelphia lawyerese.

"As soon as we're assured that shipment will really get to suffering people, we'd be glad to lift the blockade," I said, feeling a bit like a Mafia chieftan running the port. "But we understand that Pakistani soldiers are commandeering relief goods. They're using them for military operations."[1]

"You're creating unemployment and hardship in Philadelphia," he countered on another tack. "I don't see anything wrong with shipping something like tallow to Pakistan."

"What would you think about shipping tallow to Hitler's Germany at the height of World War II?" I asked.

"Well, I agree that Yahya Khan is maybe even worse than Hitler," he admitted. "But I think I'd even trade with Hitler as long as our government didn't rule it

---

1. In March, 1972, Sen. Edward Kennedy brought home the problem of shipments not reaching those in need. He charged that only a small portion of U.S. relief committed for Bangladesh actually arrived there. Over one hundred thousand tons of wheat and rice, intended for East Pakistan, for example, was diverted to West Pakistan.

illegal. As it is, you're operating completely on your own. You're conducting foreign relations!"

"I don't know how you could live with yourself if you felt you were helping Hitler," I said. "I believe people have to do what they feel is right. If it's temporarily against the law or government policy, you have to hope that government and the law will eventually catch up."

The nonviolent blockade stayed in force until Bangladesh came into being as a new nation later in the year.

An unexpected sidelight to the blockade was that six Bengali sailors, who had undoubtedly watched our protest from the *Al Ahmadi's* deck, jumped ship while the freighter was still tied up. They contacted some of the late night picketers, saying they feared for their lives on a ship where most of the crew were hostile West Pakistanis. The demonstrators contacted other Bengali and American sympathizers and took the sailors through the dark streets to private homes.

Fearful that Immigration authorities or police might catch them and force them back on the ship, we contacted the American Civil Liberties Union and, through them, an experienced immigration lawyer, Filindo Masino. With reporters hounding us for a story and with rumors of Immigration agents searching for the sailors, we scattered them to separate homes in the city and suburbs and worked out a procedure for getting them safely to the Immigration office after the *Al Ahmadi's* departure.

Mr. Masino was a skilled negotiator and the Philadelphia Immigration officials were much more sympathetic than we had expected. In a few hours of dialogue, we secured approval for the men to stay in the United States for at least a year, with permission to work and without needing visas.

During the time the ship was in port, I had several conversations with Mr. Donohue of Furness-Withy. He was furious about the ILA's refusal to load. He fumed about the line having to pay $10,000 per day to keep the ship docked. He said his New York office would call the top man in the ILA and say, "What kind of president do you have in Philadelphia anyway? How come you load ships everywhere else but here in Philly?" He also threatened a legal suit against the union.

Concerned about a possible squeeze play on Mr. Askew, I called him and related the Donohue threat.

"You don't have to worry," he said, as calm as ever. "We're used to intimidation. That doesn't bother us. I went to a meeting at the New York office and they said: 'The brass feels one way and you feel another.' I said, 'To hell with the brass.' I feel elated about the whole situation."

A few days later, Mr. Askew received a letter, signed by Ralph Bunche, Marian Anderson, and other black leaders congratulating him on his stand. Sen. Frank Church (whose office I had contacted) also sent congratulations. Sultana talked to Mr. Askew and reported that he was "tickled pink."

Not only was the action at Pier 80 covered extensively in the mass media, but national news about the situation in East Bengal was heating up. Hope twinkled in a State Department announcement that $10 million in U.S. military aid to Pakistan had "expired" and that licenses for the expired shipments would not be renewed. Sen. Edward Kennedy, Congress's most vociferous critic of American policy, called the Pakistan military action "genocide." A Toronto conference of top scholars, parliamentarians, and editors issued a "Declaration of Concern," calling the events in East Pakistan "one of the major disasters in man's history." Sen. Charles Percy, touring refugee camps, called them "one of the greatest tragedies history has ever unfolded." Alvin Toffler, writing in the August 19 *New York Times*, described the refugee camps:

I saw Indian villages deluged by masses of destitute refugees, every available inch crammed with bodies seeking shelter from the blistering sun and the torrential rain. I saw refugees still streaming along the roads unable to find even a resting place. I saw miserable Indian villagers sharing their meagre food with the latest frightened and hungry arrivals. I saw thousands of men, women and babies lined up, waiting patiently under the sun for hours to get their rations. These pitiful few ounces of rice, wheat and dahl provide a level of nutrition so low that it will inevitably create a protein breakdown, liver illness, and a variety of other diseases, in addition to the cholera, pneumonia, bronchitis that are already rampant.

Toffler excoriated what he called the moral repulsiveness of the United States, "sending still more arms to the killers," and he registered his strong protest against the "callousness and stupidity of American policy."

We talked to Tom Dine, Sen. Frank Church's legislative assistant, who told us that the Church-Saxbe Bill, which would cut off aid to Pakistan, would soon be voted on in the Foreign Relations Committee. More and more our thoughts turned to Washington, to the legislative effort, and to the possibility of bringing pressure more directly on the White House. What if we could take the suffering of the refugees and lay it directly at President Nixon's feet? Ideas were cruising around like police launches in our minds.

NOTICE OF PROPOSED DEMONSTRATION IN PARK AREA (S)
UNDER ADMINISTRATION BY NATIONAL CAPITAL PARKS,
NATIONAL PARK SERVICE, U.S. DEPARTMENT OF THE
INTERIOR.

Purpose of Proposed Demonstration: To dramatize the
suffering in E. Pakistan, to communicate at a dramatic,
symbolic location, namely the White House, and to urge
President Nixon to stop all U.S. aid to Pakistan and to
speak out against the mass killing there.

Proposed Activities Involved in Demonstration: To have
ten participants present in ten lightweight replicas of
the sewer pipes in which E. Pakistani refugees have
been forced to live in India, and to have other members
standing around this display to distribute literature,
talk to observers, and carry signs. Many of the participants may fast for varying lengths of time; some
plan to fast for ten days.

Equipment and Facilities: Ten replica sewer pipes made
of lightweight, moveable material, approximately three
feet in diameter, six to eight feet in length, with
participants spending time inside them, symbolic of the
refugees who are forced to live in these conditions in
India.

CHAPTER 7

Refugees at
the White House

The National Capital Parks Police had no desire to see
our "sewer pipe refugee camp" erected near the White
House. Hours of negotiation, letters, phone calls, and
filling out ponderous official forms produced a re-
sounding "No" from the office of William R. Failor,
Police Superintendent. We turned for advice to the
Washington office of the American Civil Liberties Union
and its fiery executive director, Ralph Temple. He secured the volunteer services of a meticulous lawyer,
James Fitzpatrick. A lower court decision went against
us, but the Appeals Court reponded to Fitzpatrick's
logic and decided that we could put our fiberboard replicas in Lafayette Park, right across Pennsylvania Avenue from the front gate of the White House.

If President Nixon read the *New York Times* on the
morning of October 14, he would have seen a story from
Dacca saying that the Pakistan government had made
East Pakistan a "place of endless horror." The report
noted, among other things, that 563 East Pakistani
women, picked up by the Pakistani army and held in
military brothels, were not being released because they
were pregnant beyond the abortion stage.

If the president had glanced across the White House
lawn toward Lafayette Park that morning, he would
have seen our newly-erected line of sewer pipes, with

the plastic sheets for rain protection stretched along the top, and the large banner, "East Pakistani Refugee Camp," hung tautly between two poles.

People came to live at the pipes from Philadelphia, Chicago, Boston, New York, and Ohio. Joan Dine, who had lived with Tom in India and who helped staff the Bangladesh Information Center, recruited local Washingtonians to join us. Some participants stayed day and night, either napping in sleeping bags inside the pipes, or sitting outside in the chill October air, handing out leaflets and chatting with curious passersby. Suki Rice, a Boston peace activist with long blond hair and blue eyes, still was able to simulate a Bengali look in a borrowed *sari*. Similarly dressed was Sue Carroll, a member of the Philadelphia Life Center, who fasted during the full ten days of her stay. Others either fasted or ate only rice, dahl, and water—the ration of the refugees.

The sacrifice was small compared with the refugees' suffering. But it gave us a sense of identification with those huddled millions who even then were seeking shelter from the monsoon. During the long, chilly nights, staring across at the White House, we wondered darkly what it must be like to feel your body wasting away, to see your bones start to protrude, to watch weaker people—children and the elderly—drop over and slip away in the flood waters.

October 15, the second day of our "camp-in," brought the encouraging news that the Senate Foreign Relations Committee had voted to adopt a slightly modified version of the Church-Saxbe Bill. The measure would cut off all economic and military assistance to Pakistan until President Nixon could certify that Pakistan was allowing the refugees to return. (The bill ultimately was included in the Foreign Assistance Act of 1971, passed by the Senate in December. Because of the controversies over foreign aid, the Act was not signed into law until February 7, 1972.)

On October 16, thirty of us marched from Lafayette

On the outskirts of Calcutta, thousands of Bengali refugees seek shelter in sewer pipes.

Sewer pipe demonstration in Washington, D.C., across from the White House.

Park to the Pakistani embassy, carrying large replicas of tanks, planes, guns, and American dollars to represent U.S. aid to Pakistan. Helmeted police stopped us five hundred feet from the embassy, explaining firmly that Washington law prohibits any demonstration closer than five hundred feet from a foreign embassy. Noting that five hundred feet from the Pakistani embassy put us directly in front of the Greek embassy, we smiled and said that we would be delighted to stay where we were and direct our "No U.S. Aid to Dictatorship" signs toward the repressive Greek regime. Finally, we negotiated a spot in a park within clear view of the Pakistan embassy.

People warned us that the jaundiced mass media of the capital are so used to demonstrations that we shouldn't expect any news stories. However the march was covered by the *Washington Post*, the *Evening Star* (with a photo), and the ABC network news. Both TV stations also had stories. Channel 7 did a broad report on the refugees in India, the possibility of war between India and Pakistan, and the establishment of our mock refugee camp in front of the White House.

On October 17 we held a religious memorial service in Lafayette Park for the victims of U.S. and Pakistan government policies. One hundred people attended, including members of the Bangladesh mission to the United Nations. It was a deeply moving experience to sit across from the White House and to reflect on those who had died and would still die, while, as we meditated, a Moslem Bengali read from the Koran, a Hindu Bengali read from the *Bhagavad-Gita,* and a Christian minister read from the Bible. At the close of the service, we passed around bowls of rice and water, a symbolic "communion" through the elements that were the refugees' rations.

On October 18 we marched to the Capitol, held a brief rally, then went inside to lobby directly with senators and representatives. On the twentieth, we invited Con-

MARCH TO THE PAKISTANI EMBASSY, WASHINGTON, D.C.

gresspeople to join us for a "refugee lunch" in Lafayette
Park behind the sewer pipes. No senators or representatives came in person, but legislative assistants from the
offices of Senators Schweiker, Church, Harris, Hatfield,
and Mikva made supportive speeches and joined in the
simple, outdoor rice and lentils meal.

We did not see the fruits of all these efforts until
two-and-a-half weeks after we dismantled the encamp-
ment and returned home. The Church-Saxbe legislation
was tied up in the Senate foreign aid debate, but congressional pressure continued to build on the Administration. Senator Kennedy kept speaking out as vocally
as before and statements critical of Administration policy were made in Congress in late October and early
November by such legislators as Bayh, Tunney,
Church, Muskie, and Frelinghuysen. On November 6,
350 American scholars and Asia experts, including five
Nobel Prize winners, called upon President Nixon to
cease all aid to Pakistan.

Dick Taylor addresses an interfaith worship service in front of the White House. This was one of the actions in Washington to call attention to U.S. support for the West Pakistani dictatorship.

There was never any official response from the White House, but the pressure got through. The November 8 *New York Times* carried the front-page story that the State Department was announcing cancellation of all licenses for export of arms to Pakistan. This completely reversed the government's position of refusing to put a full embargo on arms shipments to Pakistan. The action, according to the *Times*, finally closed the "pipeline" that had supplied arms and spare parts to Pakistan. Thus was achieved one of the major goals we had been pursuing. (The total ban on arms shipments was not eased until March 1973, long after Bangladesh achieved autonomy. It was not lifted completely until February 1975.)

Final closure was still to come, however. For months, India had been appealing to the United States to condemn the atrocities in Pakistan and to remove support from the Khan regime. The Indian government gave heroic aid to the millions of refugees, but had to cut deeply into its own much-needed economic development funds to do so. Finally, the burden became too great and on December 3, the simmering India-Pakistan conflict broke into open warfare.

The war was short. Dacca surrendered to Indian troops on December 16. A ceasefire came on the following day. On December 20, Zulfikar Ali Bhutto replaced General Khan as head of the Pakistan government. Within a few weeks, Bangladesh was an autonomous nation, ruled by the party which seemingly so long ago (though it was only a year earlier) had won the East Pakistan elections. By March 1972, nearly all the Bengali refugees had returned to their homeland.

What are the implications of all this effort? In the six years since the nonviolent fleet sailed the Delaware, I have often been called upon to tell audiences about our adventure and its significance. In my enthusiasm, I have sometimes caught myself almost claiming that we single-handedly turned around the White House, the Pentagon, and the State Department, that we "brought down the mighty from their thrones and raised up those of low degree."

It is tempting to overemphasize the impact of such an exciting campaign, which did in fact accomplish many of its goals. We have to admit, however, that we were unable to change the minds of President Nixon or Dr. Kissinger, who never spoke out publicly against the horrors committed by our ally and who, even as late as December 1971, were still trying desperately to "tilt" in favor of Pakistan. Nor could we by our actions reach out to stop the massacres, the rapes, the incredible suffering that continued for ten months. The agony of death and destruction was the background of all our efforts and did not end until the Indian army took Dacca. And, although we had a measurable impact on cutting off military aid, we never achieved our goal of eliminating economic aid to the Khan government.

It must also be said that many of the achievements that did occur came through the common work and concern of hundreds of people, many of whom were not a part of our direct action campaign. Lobbying American doctors, for example, who had done cholera research in East Pakistan, made a deep impression on congresspeople because of their intimate knowledge of the situation and their ability to refute the Administration's position. Many academicians and other prominent individuals, such as John Kenneth Galbraith, Alvin Toffler, and Mr. and Mrs. Chester Bowles, spoke out strongly and publicly against U.S. policy. Bengalis, working through the Bangladesh League of America, the Bangladesh Information Center, and like organizations, gave testimony in Congress, wrote innumerable letters, took out newspaper ads, collected funds, and otherwise supported the Bangladesh cause.

Sen. Edward Kennedy never ceased to challenge and harass the executive branch with his persistent opposition, and people like Sen. Frank Church and Rep. Cornelius Gallagher sponsored bills and kept the issue before Congress. Legislative assistants, individuals like Tom Dine, Dale de Haan, Jerry Tinker, and Mike Gertner, fed information to the legislators, provided important liaison with private groups, drafted legislation, and spoke out forcefully on their own. News reporters played a crucial role, as did the newspapers that took editorial stands against U.S. policy. In Bangladesh itself, the liberation forces, "Mukti Bahini," as they were called, kept Pakistani troops off balance, liberated significant parts of the country, and got world attention by their guerrilla actions.

Given this complex of forces, how can the impact of the nonviolent campaign be isolated and evaluated? What unique role did the Direct Action Committee play?

Seeking answers to these questions, I spent several days in Washington in the fall of 1975, talking to people who had been deeply involved in the Bangladesh issue.

I talked to Joan Dine, a striking, energetic woman, at her home in the capital. Joan is a Radcliffe graduate who once served as deputy director of recruiting for the Peace Corps. Her concern about East Bengal developed during her 1967–69 stay in India with Tom Dine, when the latter was personal assistant to Ambassador Chester Bowles. When she heard, in March 1971, that Pakistani soldiers were dropping napalm on Bengali huts, her outrage led her to agree to take on the job of coordinator of the Bangladesh Information Center, where she worked effectively for many months.

"The direct action campaign gave heart to those already involved," she told me. "We saw that through direct action we could get publicity on the issue and not just to have to work behind the scenes. It had dramatic effect that focused the issue. It carried a certain idealism that fanned the fires of enthusiasm. I think it also influenced the votes in the House and Senate. The *Padma* blockade came right before the House Foreign

Affairs Committee vote to cut off aid to Pakistan. The Church-Saxbe Bill came up for a vote when the sewer pipe city was going on. We know from our contact with staff aides that it caught the attention of people on Capitol Hill."

I also talked with Dale S. de Haan, staff director of Sen. Edward Kennedy's Refugee Subcommittee. "Well-organized direct actions dramatize an issue for people who aren't sensitive to it," he reflected. "Bangladesh didn't have a natural constituency in this country. Political change usually requires a constituency. The direct action was one of the forces that helped create the needed constituency."

Another much larger group to whom the nonviolent campaign gave heart was the Bengalis who, in 1971, were almost overwhelmed by the cataclysm befalling their country. It was delightful for me to meet again, after a four-year lapse, with some of the Bengalis with whom I had worked during that summer and fall, and to ask them how Bengalis reacted to the campaign.

The last time I had seen Mustafizur Rahman Siddiqi, now Bangladesh ambassador to the United States, was at the October 17, 1971, religious memorial service in Lafayette Park. Meeting over tea at the Bangladesh embassy on November 25, 1975, he told me: "If U.S. aid had not been cut off, the war might have continued for many years. It might have been like Vietnam. The direct action campaign helped cut off aid and focus public attention. Your contribution was immensely valuable."

Mr. Siddiqi's press consul, Syed Nuruddin Munaim, told me how the blockades looked from Bangladesh itself. In 1971, he was a newspaperman living in Dacca, surreptitiously feeding news items to foreign correspondents at the Intercontinental Hotel.

"When we heard of the ship blockade, there was absolute jubilation, sir," he told me. "Those were very dark days, very hopeless days. The newspapers were all censored, but we listened to BBC, All-India Radio, and the clandestine Bangladesh Liberation Radio. One of them told of your efforts. The news of the blockade spread like wildfire. Even in the villages people heard of it."

Mr. Nuruddin spoke of how he travelled to small rural villages. "The villagers said joyfully, 'The American government is sending arms to our enemies, but the American people won't allow the arms to leave the port,' " he said. "The feeling generated was that while the U.S. government was against us, the working people of the U.S., the common people, were sympathetic to us. It was a great boost."

Sultan Ahmad, who now works at the World Bank, but who in 1971 participated in the campaign while studying for a Ph.D. in economics, also found that news of the blockade was widespread in Bangladesh. He returned to his homeland in 1972 and 1973, and talked to many people, curious to see if the actions in which he participated had had any impact. He found that the blockade was widely known. Often he got the reaction: "We know the American people were behind us."

"People in Bangladesh were surprised," he told me over lunch at the International Monetary Fund office. "They didn't expect so much. They didn't think Americans would seek to share, to simulate their suffering. There was a tremendous feeling of identity and gratitude."

To the south of Bangladesh, Indians were also much affected by the campaign. They bitterly resented what seemed to them U.S. support for genocide and they cheered any initiatives by Americans to turn around the Nixon-Kissinger policy. When Charles Walker visited India in September 1971, he found that the nonviolent fleet's exploits had been carried prominently in the Indian press. He was always applauded by audiences when he was introduced as one of the organizers of the *Padma* project.

When Radhakrishnan, a prominent philosopher, follower of Gandhi, and former president of India, visited

Jack Patterson in 1972, he pumped Jack continuously for information about the Baltimore action against the *Padma*. He said that the Indian Gandhians were greatly cheered when they heard of the action, as it was the first sign of a positive American response to the crisis.

There are also indications that the ship blockade actually saved lives by preventing the loading of some equipment and by delaying ships. It was the Direct Action Committee that played the crucial role of gaining the support of the ILA and, through collaboration with Richard Askew's local, closed the port of Philadelphia to Pakistani ships.

"There is no doubt that it did help reduce the supply of arms and related goods," says Muhammad Bhuiyan, who was active in the 1971 campaign and now works for the International Monetary Fund. "I went back to the dock a year after the *Al Ahmadi* left Philadelphia and found its shipment still lying on the pier. When the *Al Ahmadi* left, it had to go, not only without its Philadelphia cargo, but also without part of its crew. It must have been a blow to the Pakistani military's morale to have ships arrive late, with only part of their agreed-upon cargo and only part of the crew."

I know of at least four freighters where Bengali crewmen jumped ship. They told us hair-raising tales of life on board, as when the majority West Pakistani crew threatened to knife them and throw them overboard. Bengali seamen whose ships returned to West Pakistan were often interned, and there were rumors of killings of Bengalis in Karachi. It seems clear, therefore, that lives were saved here too when the Direct Action Committee helped Bengali sailors get off the ships.

One of the major impacts of the campaign, of course, was its educational role. When confronted by an appalling injustice, the ordinary person is often at a loss to know what to do. Others are often uniformed and apathetic. There seems no way to get the concern before a broader public. What the ship-blocking campaign did was to give a small group of concerned people a platform from which they could spread their concern beyond their own circle and out to the general public. Newspapers not only covered the actions, but usually carried quotes from the participants. Direct Action Committee members were interviewed dozens of times on radio and TV. Stories were even carried in the global press, including, we found, the *Times of India.*

The drama of the actions had a special appeal for television. Often coverage of the nonviolent fleet was used as a pretext for broader stories on government policy and the East Pakistan situation. Thus, the attention of millions of viewers was captured, and they were informed of the role of their country in supporting the Pakistani army's atrocities.

Nor was this coverage occasional or passing. The constant reiteration of direct action "sociodramas" kept the issue of aid to Pakistan before the mass media and did not allow it to be shelved. As I found in my talk with Tad Szulc, newspapers won't repeat the same story, "Pakistani Ships Carry U.S. Arms," over and over. As Szulc said, "It just isn't news." But the direct action campaign took this simple fact and made it into news day after day, thus undercutting the government's rationalizations and evasions and increasing the pressure for a changed policy. It also, Joan Dine believes, contributed to the growing consciousness among Americans who more and more question whether U.S. aid should be used in support of *any* dictatorships.

A final accomplishment of the Direct Action Committee was to develop a new form of citizen direct action. As far as I know, the nonviolent fleet is the first instance in American history of citizens protesting U.S. foreign policy by an unarmed blockade of foreign ships. In June 1971, Sen. Frank Church had urged President Nixon to order the U.S. Coast Guard to intercept the *Padma* and prevent the delivery of its military equipment. The president, of course, did not. But the the Direct Action Committee *did* intercept the *Padma* and, later, other ships. Instead of waiting helplessly for the government to act, or simply writing irate letters, the Committee acted directly. It was able to close completely two ports (Philadelphia and Boston) to Pakistani shipping and to make a significant contribution to changing U.S. policy.

In the following chapter, I want to focus on how nonviolent direct action can help confront today's enormous injustices. Of the many examples that could be mentioned, I will cite just three areas in which direct action can be applied: one dealing with U.S. support for repressive governments, one based in a local neighborhood but relating to the global hunger crisis, and one concerned with the national-level problem of nuclear power plants.

*Demonstrators erect a "torture tableau"
(designed by the social justice group "Liberty to
the Captives") to call attention to U.S.
support for repressive governments.*

CHAPTER 8

Nonviolent Struggle in Today's World

The most obvious kind of campaign that flows from the foregoing chapters of this book is the struggle to change U.S. foreign policy and to support Third World movements for human liberation by challenging the current U.S. support for dictatorships and oppressive oligarchies. Blocking ships in U.S. ports is certainly not the only means of waging such struggle, but it is fascinating to think what it would mean if every Chilean, or Brazilian, or Rhodesian, or South African ship that came to U.S. ports were greeted by a nonviolent blockade similar to that used in the Pakistan campaign of 1971. Wouldn't this be an effective means to put on the national agenda the question of U.S. involvement in torture, apartheid, and dictatorship? Wouldn't this be a way to communicate to oppressed people suffering under dictatorial regimes the same message that Bengalis received in 1971: "The American government may be supporting our enemies, but the American people are for us"?

The range of possible nonviolent campaigns is immense. Dr. Gene Sharp, who has devoted most of his adult life to the study of nonviolence, has published a monumental study listing hundreds of different kinds of

nonviolent movements throughout history and out-
lining 198 separate kinds of nonviolent action (*The Politics of Nonviolent Action* [Boston: Porter Sargent,
1973]). The challenge, it seems to me, is to use creative
imagination to project nonviolent strategies onto the
major injustices we face and to start organizing.

To illustrate, here are just three scenarios of possible
nonviolent campaigns.[1]

PROBLEM

*The United States supports—with military and eco-
nomic aid, private investment, and sometimes with the
CIA—dictatorships and ruling oligarchies that use torture and other repressive means to secure their power.*[2]

SCENARIO

A group calling itself "Christians and Jews against
Torture and Dictatorship" organize a two-week march
from New York City to Washington, D.C. They carry
large, blown-up photos of political prisoners who have

---

1. A "scenario," as used here, is a fictionalized account written to
portray how an action might unfold. As of this writing, the scenarios
given here have never happened in the past. They are presented as
illustrations of what might happen in the future. Obviously, I feel that
nonviolent ship-blocking has enormous potential as a campaign. I
have not given a ship-blocking scenario, however, since the earlier
chapters give, I hope, a clear picture of how such a campaign could be
organized. The above scenarios are taken, with substantial expansion
and changes, from my article, "The Peacemakers," which appeared in
the October-November 1975 issue of *Post-American*.

2. A glaring example of U.S. support for a torture-practicing dictatorship is the case of Brazil. U.S. diplomacy toward Brazil has been
characterized by "friendship, esteem and affection" (see *New York
Times*, March 15, 1974) ever since a 1964 coup brought a military junta
to power. A U.S. "public assistance safety program" has trained over
one hundred thousand Brazilian police, post-1964 economic aid has
been about $2 billion, one of the largest Latin American military

been tortured in the jails of Chile, Brazil, South Africa, and other nations aided by the United States. They also carry signs saying, "End All U.S. Support for Torture and Dictatorship." As they pass through various towns in New Jersey, Pennsylvania, Delaware, and Maryland, they set up street corner rallies where they do soap-box speaking and leafleting of the center-city crowds, explaining how the U.S. is defending democracy at home and dictatorship overseas.

They arrive at the Capitol building on the opening day of Congress and unroll a large banner saying: "I Cannot Endure Iniquity and Solemn Assembly—Isaiah 1:31." Dressed in costumes representing the military and police of the various dictatorships the U.S. supports, they announce to the press that they will open a "Torture Information Center" in a storefront office between the Capitol and the White House. They hand out information that will be available at the Center, e.g., leaflets

---

missions of the U.S. is in Brazil, and American corporations are heavily involved in the economy.

The repressive nature of the Brazilian regime is highlighted by its extensive use of torture to silence opposition. Even priests and nuns have not been immune to torture by the police. Many Americans were made aware of this by an article in *Harper's Magazine* (October 1975) in which Fred Morris, an American Methodist missionary, described being tortured with beatings and electric shocks by Brazilian police. Amnesty International's 1972 document, *Report on Allegations of Torture in Brazil*, cited manifold types of torture, including the horror of prisoners being forced to watch the torture of friends and family. Amnesty's "World Survey of Torture" said that in Brazil torture is "widespread" and can be said to constitute "administrative practice" (see Amnesty International, *Report on Torture* [New York: Farrar, Straus and Giroux, 1975], p. 199).

The same pattern of U.S. military and economic aid to repressive governments can be found in our relations with such governments as Chile, the Philippines, South Korea, Guatemala, and Indonesia. In case after case, U.S. policy has been similar to the support given Pakistan in 1971. Sen. Alan Cranston of California, in fact, has estimated that 75 percent of the countries receiving U.S. aid have repressive regimes. For many of these governments, U.S diplomatic, economic, and military support is a key element keeping them in power.

showing the specifics of U.S. support for particular regimes, Amnesty International reports on torture, drafts
of legislation to end U.S. relations with repressive governments. They invite TV, radio, and the newspapers to
cover the direct action that will follow.

CJTD designates Wednesday as "End Torture Day."
Making clear the project's nonviolent discipline, they
invite clergy, peace and religious groups, students, un-
ions, feminist organizations, and other concerned people to participate.

On the first Wednesday, they march from their Center
to the White House, carrying an "exhibit" showing the
"pau de arrara," a specific method of torture used in
Brazil. At the White House, they form a vigil line and
hold up signs showing photos of people who have been
tortured in Brazil. The "exhibit," a mock torture room,
is placed on the sidewalk in front of the White House.
Several of the marchers, using a dummy, demonstrate
to the press and passersby how the particular method of
torture is used. One page affidavits from people who
have been tortured in Brazil are handed out.

An American missionary, who was tortured in Brazil,
gives a speech describing his experience. A rabbi speaks,
citing the parallel between Brazil and Nazi Germany.
Leaflets are handed out describing the police-military-
aid-investment relation of the U.S. to Brazil, and calling
for action by the president to bring an end to such backing. After an hour's silent vigil, a local clergyman gives a
closing prayer, asking God's help in letting "justice roll
down like waters and righteousness like an ever-flowing
stream." The marchers return to their Center.

On each subsequent Wednesday, similar marches and
vigils are held, with "exhibits" showing well-known torture methods—the electric prod, the "submarine," the
"sawhorse," the "grill," etc.—used in other countries
supported by the U.S. The weekly demonstrations are
held, not only at the White House, but also at Congress,
various foreign embassies, Fort McNair (one location

where foreign military personnel receive U.S. training), and the CIA building in Langley, Virginia. A CJTD recruiting team contacts a wide spectrum of sympathetic groups, particularly from the religious community, and gets them involved in the marches.

On the last day of the campaign, a mass march is held from the White House to the Capitol. There, all the various torture exhibits are lined up in a row and the torture apparatuses demonstrated. After speeches and prayers, the marchers go into the Senate and House to lobby with their representatives for legislative action to remove all U.S. support from torture and torture-practicing regimes.

PROBLEM

Unplanned urban sprawl in the United States removes about a million acres a year from agriculture. Speculators and developers make fortunes from land appreciation. Thousands of food-producing farms disappear at a time when half a billion of the world's people are hungry.

SCENARIO

The congregation of an inner-city church, most of whose members live in the surrounding low-income neighborhood, form a committee to study the world food crisis. Because their parish has many poor people, they are aware that hunger exists locally as well as in countries like Bangladesh. They decide that some dramatic action is needed to call attention to the misplaced priorities that bury food-producing land under concrete while millions of humans are starving. They organize a series of well-publicized neighborhood meetings to share their concern with local people. At each meeting, direct action plans are discussed and interested people invited to nonviolent training workshops.

The action which begins their summer-long campaign takes place on a neighborhood street where a child was struck by a speeding auto. House-to-house visits have shown a high degree of interest in the church group's concern about world hunger, and also in safer streets and a better environment.

The press is invited and told that a dramatic "street closing ceremony" will take place on a given Saturday. When the TV cameras arrive, they find the street sealed off with a barricade made up of large photos of the world's hungry. Several members of the congregation are pounding away at the street surface with a rented jackhammer. Other members are lifting out broken pieces of roadway and piling them neatly along the sidewalk. Farther back, where the earth has been uncovered, other members are turning over the hard-packed soil with garden tools and starting to plant a vegetable garden. Others are carrying signs with sayings like, "Pour Yourself Out for the Hungry," and "I Was Hungry and You Fed Me." They hand out a leaflet that reads:

Streets, parking lots, and garages take up one-third of our city space. The spread of our cities, suburbs, and highways removes two acres of agricultural land every minute. Our nation must repent of the practices that line the pockets of speculators and pave over arable land to serve gas-guzzling, steel-consuming, polluting automobiles, while millions of God's children starve for lack of bread.

We deplore the existence of widespread hunger here in this richest of nations. We urge the conversion of city streets to gardens, bike paths, and decent mass transit. We urge a radical cut-back on auto production to free petroleum and other resources for the fertilizer, tractors, and irrigation systems so desperately needed by poor countries. We urge a national commitment to end hunger in America and to create the international mechanisms to end hunger everywhere in the world.

Let us not be like those infamous cities of biblical times that God removed because they had "surfeit of food and prosperous ease, but did not aid the poor and the needy" (Ezekiel 16:49).

PROBLEM

American energy-producing corporations are heavily committed to nuclear power as a means of generating electricity. They claim that atomic power is a source of limitless, safe energy to meet America's burgeoning needs. In actual fact, nuclear power is one of the most dangerous technologies ever developed. While much desired as a money-maker by private utilities, nuclear energy is not needed and could be replaced by conservation measures and alternative energy sources, like solar power.

SCENARIO

The Washington Power and Light Company spends $2 million to build and equip an exhibit building near the site of their proposed atomic energy electric generating plant. The exhibit purports to show the "safety" of nuclear power and urges reliance on the nuclear approach to meet energy needs.

An ecology action group, "Power for People," creates an alternate exhibit at a nearby farmhouse. Sympathetic engineers and artists help them put together working models, diagrams, and films to show the dangers of nuclear power. One model shows what happens when the "emergency core cooling system" fails, spewing lethal radiation into the atmosphere. Another demonstrates the "China syndrome," in which the reactor's overheated core sinks white-hot into the earth, venting cancer-producing radiation up through cracks to the surface. One section of the exhibit leads the viewer through the many government-industry plans—first accepted, then abandoned—for disposing of poisonous radioactive wastes produced by atomic plants. It shows that no one knows how to deal with these cancer-producing agents, some of which will be highly dangerous for thousands of years.

The farmhouse not only has an exhibit of alternative

sources of power which could be substituted for the nuclear approach, but its own lighting and heating is provided by windmills and solar collectors. The house is also
used as a nonviolent training center. Visitors are given
information about training workshops. Other trainees
are recruited from nearby colleges and existing ecology
groups. Speakers also go out to local churches and community groups, explaining the dangers of a nuclear
power plant in the area. House-to-house leafleting and
discussions also inform people.

Early in the nonviolent campaign, vigils are held at
the entrance of the plant site; leaflets are distributed to
the surveyors and other workers. On the day that actual
construction is to begin, one hundred members of
"Power for People" stand in line across the plant's entrance, holding hands and blocking the trucks carrying
construction materials. They hand out a statement saying that their clasped hands "represent the fragile links
that bind the ecosystem and make life possible. Nuclear
plants like this," the statement reads,"poison the earth,
destroy life, and ruin the world for future generations."

Several demonstrators are arrested, but TV coverage
brings out more demonstrators on the following day.
People from surrounding towns, whose concern about
safety has been raised, also arrive and give support.
Within two weeks, there are a thousand demonstrators
in front of the plant gate and the state legislature is
reeling from protests by concerned residents who are
insisting that construction be stopped.[3]

---

3. A scenario showing such growth in support may seem fanciful, but
during 1975 a nonviolent action group in Switzerland organized an
action similar to the above which, on one day, brought out fifteen
thousand people to occupy the site of a proposed nuclear plant near
Basel. The occupation was so successful that police could not evict the
demonstrators, who set up sleeping and eating quarters on the property. Eventually, the Swiss government had to begin negotiations
with opponents of nuclear power in Switzerland about the whole future of the Swiss nuclear program.

Publicity in the mass media brings many inquiries from other parts of the nation where nuclear plants are being built. "Power for People" decides to organize a travelling training team to go around the country giving nonviolent direct action workshops and encouraging campaigns similar to theirs. "Our main goal," they say, "is to gain a moratorium on nuclear plant construction in the United States. But we will also educate people about the need to take the control of energy out of the hands of big oil companies and private utilities and put it under the control of electric co-ops or municipally-owned companies run by democratically-elected boards. Energy should be developed by and for the people, not by and for the corporations."

An earlier book, which I helped write, shows how a large number of direct action campaigns, such as those described in the above scenarios, could be linked together with a political strategy to qualitatively transform American society as a whole.[4]

The book asks the basic question: Can we ever solve our domestic problems and act with some modicum of justice in international affairs so long as our economic system channels the preponderant wealth and power to a small, capital-owning elite and so long as economic life is based on the acquisitive impulse to private enrichment rather than on promotion of the common good? It puts forward an alternative vision of an economic system based on democracy, ecological harmony, physical security, equality, and social ownership of capital. Whether one's hopes are so "revolutionary," or whether one has a more limited aim of "reforming" specific struc-

---

4. Susanne Gowan, George Lakey, William Moyer, and Richard Taylor, *Moving toward a New Society* (Philadelphia: New Society Press, 1976). See also George Lakey, *Strategy for a Living Revolution* (New York: Grossman, 1973).

tures within the existing political economy, nonviolent direct action can be a powerful tool.

In this post-Vietnam war period, when mass non-violent action is the exception rather than the rule, it is encouraging to see the development of a growing number of groups from coast to coast commited to nonviolent campaign-building. Some are large and well-known, like Cesar Chavez's United Farm Workers. Others, like the Community for Creative Nonviolence, in Washington, D.C., are relatively small, local groups committed to risk-taking, prophetic action in a nonviolent spirit.

At a broader level, the Movement for a New Society, with which I am connected, is a transnational network of action groups working for a transformed social order through nonviolent strategies which include direct action, simple living communities, "Macro-Analysis Seminars," and alternative institutions. There are also study and training centers, like the Philadelphia Life Center and the Institute for the Study of Nonviolence in California, that give concerned people the competence to engage in effective nonviolent struggle. All of these networks relate to more long-established groups, like the Fellowship of Reconciliation, the War Resisters League, the American Friends Service Committee, and the Catholic Worker Movement, whose long experience in nonviolent direct action is an invaluable resource.

Finally, there are many groups, such as the People's Bicentennial Commission, that, while not using the explicit term "nonviolence" to describe their strategies, nevertheless use creative nonviolent demonstrations in their work to change society.

This movement is still relatively small by the world's standards, but it is a sign of hope that we can struggle effectively for social justice while, as Daniel Berrigan put it, "avoiding like the plague the plague we are seeking to destroy."

PART TWO

NONVIOLENT
DIRECT ACTION:
A MANUAL

Dom Helder Camara, Roman Catholic Bishop in Brazil, advocates nonviolent action in the struggle for social and economic justice.

Nonviolent Direct Action

I hope that the story of the "nonviolent fleet" and the other actions around the Pakistan issue give the reader a sense of how a nonviolent campaign can develop. An overall nonviolent campaign, however, is made up of a series of interlinked nonviolent actions taking place on a day-to-day basis. Often I hear the question: "How do you actually organize a direct action project? What are the nuts and bolts of putting together a demonstration? How would I go about it if I wanted to challenge some social injustice through nonviolent action?"

I have a feeling that people often do not engage in direct action, not because they are unwilling, but because they think they don't know how. Or because they think that nonviolent struggle requires the charisma of a Gandhi or a Martin Luther King.

This "manual" section of the book gives, I hope, a clear, step-by-step method that *any* committed person can follow in developing a direct action campaign. My hope is that people will use it to mount effective challenges to the structures that lock so many of the world's people into poverty, hunger, and oppression.

One caution: A "manual" is always a bit artificial. Like life itself, a direct action campaign is complex, full of the unexpected. You cannot entirely program it or plan for every contingency. It requires "art" and

creativity along with planning. And hard work is a crucial ingredient for success.

There is nothing sacred, therefore, in the steps listed
below or in the order in which they are given. They
cannot cover every possible contingency. They provide a
range of tools and methods, and it is a rare direct action
campaign that uses all of them. So use the ones that
seem best in your local situation, and ignore the others.
Feel free to juggle or interweave the steps as seems
appropriate. Look on what follows as a general method
that organizers of nonviolent action, here and in other
countries, have found useful.[1]

One other word. I will never forget the comment that
Bernard Lafayette, one of Martin Luther King's closest
associates, made to me when we were talking about how
to resolve difficult problems that sometimes arise in
demonstrations.

"If you're really motivated by love for people," he said,
"you'll tend to come up with the right action." That is
important to keep in mind as we consider the "method"
of nonviolent action.

---

1. In putting together the manual, I have drawn on my twenty-plus
years of experience in direct action. This included over a year spent on
the staff of Martin Luther King's Southern Christian Leadership
Conference, involvement at an organizing level with many antiwar
demonstrations, and five years at the Philadelphia Life Center, a
training center for nonviolent action.

I have also consulted with many others who have done direct action
organizing, both here and abroad. I have also reviewed books on nonviolence and manuals written for specific action projects.

I want to give particular credit to the very useful *Organizer's Manual*, put out by the War Resisters League (339 Lafayette Street, New
York, NY 10012). from which a number of ideas in this chapter were
drawn. It should also be noted that this chapter follows the outline of
an article I wrote entitled "A Manual for Nonviolent Direct Action,"
which appeared in the *Post-American*, November 1974, pp. 24–29.

SUMMARY OF THE
STEP-BY-STEP DIRECT ACTION METHOD

STEP I   THINK THROUGH PERSONAL COMMITMENT

STEP II   GET IN TOUCH WITH OTHERS:
              DEVELOP A CORE GROUP

A. Involving People: Some Suggestions

B. Keeping Things Straight: A Notebook

C. Achieving a Good Group Spirit:
   Suggestions

STEP III INVESTIGATE

A. Investigative Methods: Fact-Finding

B. Preparing a Resource File

C. Not Getting Stuck

STEP IV   STRATEGIZE

A. Setting Clear Goals

B. Writing a Strategic Plan

C. Writing a Scenario and/or Time Line

D. Keeping in Mind What Makes Nonviolent
   Direct Action Work

E. Developing a Draft Proposal, an Action
   Plan

STEP V   NEGOTIATE

A. Preparing Ahead of Time

B. The Negotiation Session Itself

C. After the Negotiation Session

117

STEP VI   EDUCATE

STEP VII ORGANIZE
        A. Expanding the Group
        B. Holding Meetings of the Expanded Group
        C. Deciding on Specific Tasks

STEP VIII TRAIN FOR DEMONSTRATIONS
        A. The Role-Play
        B. Quick Decision
        C. Situation Analysis
        D. Hassle Lines

STEP IX   APPEAL

STEP X   DEMONSTRATE
        A. A Few Days before the Demonstration
        B. On Demonstration Day
        C. At the Demonstration
        D. Dealing with Provocation or Violence
        E. Ending the Demonstration

STEP XI   BUILD A LONG-TERM CAMPAIGN

STEP I: THINK THROUGH PERSONAL COMMITMENT

When you first become concerned about an issue of social injustice, you need time for reflection before jump-
ing into action. Some questions to ask yourself: Do I
really know the facts? Am I rushing off half-cocked? Am
I prepared to take the risks that nonviolent action may
involve? What restrictions are put on me by time,
energy, knowledge, ability, other commitments? If I become involved in a direct action campaign, how can I
cover my other responsibilities, e.g., for work, for family? For the religious person: Is this just a "good idea" of
mine, or is this something God wants me to do?

STEP II: GET IN TOUCH WITH OTHERS: DEVELOP A CORE GROUP

At the center of the best nonviolent action is a core of
people who are committed to one another and to over-
coming the social evil in question. Perhaps a group
committed to nonviolent struggle is already in existence
(e.g., a local United Farm Workers group picketing
supermarkets) and all you need do is join them. If not,
you need to contact others, share your concern with
them, and see if they would like to work together.

An initial group may be only three or four people.
Rarely is it good to have more than ten or twelve in the
early stages, as this is a time for searching together,
developing group cohesion and purpose, defining tentative goals and strategies for the project. When clarity of
direction is achieved, more people can be drawn in.

A. Involving People: Some Suggestions

1. Make a list of potentially interested people and
groups (friends, social action-oriented groups, etc.) and
talk to them.

2. Make copies of a good article about the injustice. Pass them out to people. Ask for their reactions and ask if they would like to do something about it.

3. Write up and circulate a brief proposal on the issue and your initial action ideas.

4. Call a small group meeting to discuss the issue.

5. Get an invitation to speak at a potentially interested group. Have some literature to hand out. There may be a film you can show that highlights the injustice. Well-known outside speakers are sometimes available.

B. *Keeping Things Straight: A Notebook*

1. Some people try to organize direct action out of their hip pocket. They put down phone numbers on slips of paper that get lost. They get confused about what they decided three meetings ago.

2. An extremely useful organizer's tool is a small, 6" x 9½" looseleaf notebook, divided into such sections as: Press Contacts, Names and Phones of Supporters, Daily Journal and Meeting Minutes, Strategy Ideas, Police, and Research.

3. Some uses for the notebook:

   a. Jogging your memory about decisions made at earlier meetings.

   b. Remembering the names of the many people who flow through a direct action project.

   c. Having names and phone numbers of potential demonstrators close at hand so you can contact them quickly for actions.

   d. Having information for speeches readily available.

   e. If you end up going to court: remembering what happened weeks or months later when you go to trial.

C. *Achieving a Good Group Spirit: Suggestions*

1. Maximize the group's creative energy. Be sensitive to group process.

a. Don't let one or two people dominate. Encourage everyone to speak up, participate, take responsibility. Rotate roles, e.g., facilitating meetings, mimeographing leaflets.

b. Counter sexism and racism. Work for an atmosphere where women and minority group members feel free to participate fully, and where everyone can be gentle, affectionate, and playful, as well as strong, competent, and capable of leadership.

c. Try consensus decision-making.

d. Don't railroad decisions. Have a goal and tentative agenda for meetings, but let the group review the agenda and make their own additions and changes. Try putting agreed-upon time limits on each agenda item so that everyone's point will be covered. Naming a "time-keeper" may help move things along.

e. Use a flipchart that everyone can see to list the agenda, jot down brainstorming ideas, write jobs that need doing. This gives a sense of clarity, accomplishment, and forward motion to the group. Rather than talking into the air, everyone can see agenda items being ticked off, responsibilities being assumed, etc.

f. Welcome new people and get them involved.

g. Share exciting things happening in your lives.[2]

h. Evaluate your meetings at the end. A process the Philadelphia Life Center has found helpful is to put the following on a flip-chart:

---

2. At the Philadelphia Life Center we often begin meetings with "good's and new's" or "excitement sharing"—giving people time to tell about things in the last few days or week that have really grabbed them, turned them on. This gets meetings off on a positive, enthusiastic note and helps us know one another, not just in terms of the immediate task, but in terms of many dimensions of our lives.

+	—	$\longrightarrow$
(In this space goes a list of things people LIKED about the meeting.)	(In this space goes a list of things people felt could BE IMPROVED.)	(Here we list SPECIFIC SUGGESTIONS for improving the next meeting.)

Evaluation gives people a practical way to get out gripes and to work together to constantly improve the quality of meetings.

2. Give people lots of trust, validation, affirmation.

3. Have fun. Celebrate. Enjoy. Take time for singing. Take breaks. Have a potluck meal together. Learn some "light and livelies."[3] If you're a religious group, do creative worship. Pray together. Build in Bible study. Praise the Lord!

4. Deepen your nonviolent commitment.

   a. Your group may draw in people with no experience in nonviolent action and deep questions about its relevance or their personal ability to practice nonviolence. Even people with experience need to deepen their understanding and commitment.

   b. Some suggestions:

   1) Do some common study. The writings of Gandhi and Martin Luther King are especially relevant. The last

---

3. The Friends Peace Committee's booklet, *For the Fun of It* (F.P.C., 1501 Cherry Street, Philadelphia, Pa. 19102, March 1975) lists dozens of cooperative games that can be interspread through meetings to loosen them up, get people sharing, undercut tension.

Singing is a good way to build group spirit.
This "street ministry" took place at the Campaign
for Global Justice's 1976 demonstrations
at the Eucharistic Congress, Philadelphia.

chapter of George Lakey's *Strategy for a Living Revolution* has an excellent rundown of answers to the objections most commonly raised against nonviolence.

2) Rent or borrow a film. There are fine movies on nonviolence, showing how campaigns for the rights of farm workers, women, black people, etc., were organized.

3) Ask people who join you to make a practical commitment to nonviolence. It's not necessary that everyone in the project have a deep philosophical commitment, but it *is* important that all be willing to at least experiment with nonviolent methods during the life of the campaign. Such experimentation often leads to deeper commitment.

4) Don't argue too much about the philosophy of nonviolence. Show that it's the most effective strategy to

achieve the project's goals. A nonviolent stance most often comes, not just from commitment to its theory, but from answering the question: "Will this proposed tactic help or hinder us in achieving our objectives?"

STEP III: INVESTIGATE

The first task of the core group is to make sure that its facts are correct. How can you substantiate the charge that people are being tortured in the jails of Chile? What are the exact ways in which the U.S. government supports overseas dictatorships? In what way is plutonium dangerous to human life?

You can't have *all* the facts before acting, but you should be reasonably sure of an accurate account of the problem before tackling it.

A. Investigative Methods: Fact-Finding

1. Separate facts from rumors and fuzzy information. A campaign based on false or shaky facts is beaten from the start.

2. Use the research method appropriate to your issue: for example, interviews with knowledgeable people or organizations, observation, library research, questionnaires, personal experience.

B. Preparing a Resource File

As you collect information, put relevant newspaper articles, reports, books, etc., in a central file for the group, readily available for speakers, press releases, etc.

C. Not Getting Stuck

Beware of the "paralysis of analysis." Research can be an excuse for inaction. Get the facts you need, but move ahead on the injustice.

STEP IV: STRATEGIZE

A "strategy" is a general course of action selected to achieve your goals. Once you have the facts together, you need to think concretely about what steps your group can take to confront the unjust situation. Here are some useful methods of strategizing. Remember, strategies will probably have to be revised as you go along.

A. Setting Clear Goals

1. Spend part of a meeting discussing: "What's the aim of this campaign? What would we like to have happen as a result of our effort? Where would we like to be in six months with regard to this issue?" See if you can list a few simple, clearly stated goals. Having them is very helpful in explaining the project to new people and to the public, keeping action focused, and evaluating what is being accomplished as the project unfolds.

2. Keep goals concrete. "To make the world a better place" is a great goal, but it's a bit *too* general to focus action around. The goals of the "Peoples' Blockade" (which attempted to block ammunition ships and trains carrying weapons to Vietnam by holding worship services on the tracks and paddling canoes in front of war vessels) were "(1) try to slow or stop ammunition shipments; (2) help soldiers and sailors who are opposed to the war; (3) put a public spotlight on the shipments; and (4) inspire similar actions around the country." After four months of effort, every goal of the campaign was achieved (especially 2, 3 and 4), and participants could look back on the campaign with a deep feeling of accomplishment.

B. Writing a Strategic Plan

1. A "Strategic Plan" is a statement of the underlying assumptions of a campaign or project, the objectives

sought, the overall strategy to be employed, and the specific tactics and tasks that must be undertaken to implement the strategy. It helps organizers think very concretely about where they are going and how they plan to get there.

2. We did not write a strategic plan for the Pakistani campaign, but if we had, our initial one might have looked like this:

Assumptions: (1) The West Pakistani government is committing near-genocide on the people of East Pakistan. (2) The American government, while denying involvement, is actually supplying the West Pakistani regime with arms and economic aid.

Goals: (1) End U.S. support for West Pakistan until the army is withdrawn, the refugees allowed to return, and democracy restored. (2) Educate the American public about U.S. support for dictatorships.

Strategy: Develop a series of dramatic direct actions that will put a public spotlight on U.S. shipments to Pakistan and will pressure the government to cut off its support.

Tactics: (1) Organize a nonviolent canoe blockade of Pakistani ships. (2) Picket companies handling the ships. (3) Work for the maximum publicity of the situation.

Tasks: (Here would be listed the jobs that need doing: finding canoes, handling press contacts, writing leaflets, making signs, etc.)

C. Writing a Scenario and/or Time Line

1. Write a futuristic, fictionalized scenario (such as those given in chapter 8) showing how various actions might hang together and move toward the group's goals. This helps clarify what is realistic, what is likely to work and not work. It gets people thinking creatively about the range of strategies and tactics that might be used to accomplish the group's goals.

2. A "time line" can be written independently or can flow from a scenario. It simply means writing down in very specific terms what will have to happen, day by day, week by week, month by month, if the group's projected goals are to be reached. A time line is especially useful if it is put on a big chart (with weeks or months down the left-hand side and tasks listed beside each) and hung where everyone can see it.

D. *Keeping in Mind What Makes Nonviolent Direct Action Work*

1. A classic American example of effective direct action was the lunch counter sit-ins originally organized by black students in the South. The act of sitting-in showed the determination of black people to have equal service. It undercut the myth that they were "happy" with segregation. It painted a vivid picture which didn't require a complicated explanation to get across its point.

2. Here are some key elements that help make nonviolent action effective:

a. The action educates the public by painting a clear, dramatic picture of the injustice and the fallacy of the rationalizations used to cover it up.

b. The action appeals to widely-held values (e.g., in a democracy, everyone should have a right to vote; Americans shouldn't support torture or dictatorships; "Thou shalt not kill").

c. The action has momentum and builds toward a climax (e.g., Gandhi's salt march, the build-up toward the blockade of the *Padma*).

d. The participants are willing to sacrifice for what they believe.

e. The participants show creative goodwill toward all opponents.

f. The action is not "one-shot"; it is sustained over weeks or months.

g. The action is direct, not indirect. It makes a

straightforward assault on the injustice through protest (picketing, etc.) or head-on intervention (e.g., ship-blocking).

h. The action involves noncooperation with injustice (e.g., the Longshoremen's refusal to load Pakistani ships).

i. The action gives people an opportunity to do something constructive to show their concern (e.g., write your congressperson, don't buy scab lettuce).

j. The action offers an alternative, a constructive solution by which the injustice can be overcome (e.g., symbolized by black people standing in line to vote).

3. Charles Walker, who participated in the Pakistani campaign, summarizes nonviolent action as: "An amalgam of noncooperation and withdrawal of consent along with the organized impact of a nonviolent assault on a power position, the spiritual power of openness and goodwill toward opponents, and a willingness to take risks for what you believe."

E. Developing a Draft Proposal, an Action Plan

1. Write a brief proposal telling what you plan to do. The "strategic plan" format is a good one to make clear what you want to do and how you intend to go about it.

2. Duplicate the proposal and use it in recruiting others.

STEP V: NEGOTIATE

Sometimes negotiations are not appropriate or necessary. But often a group's study will reveal a specific individual or group who, if they were willing, could eliminate or substantially reduce the social evil in question. The manager of the supermarket chain *could* change policy and refuse to carry scab grapes and lettuce. The slumlord *could* agree to fix up the dilapidated apartment house.

If such policy-makers can be located, try to meet with

them to see if they can be persuaded to change. Don't assume that perpetrators of injustice are necessarily beyond appeals to reason or morality. There are cases in which unjust situations have been resolved through negotiation rather than confrontation.

Be careful, though, not to be taken in by vague promises, friendly but evasive statements, or public relations "snow jobs." Government agencies and businesses are skilled at handling citizen and customer complaints. Many a negotiation team has imagined they made progress, when in reality they came away empty-handed. To avoid this:

A. *Preparing Ahead of Time*

1. Write out and agree upon a list of demands or a statement saying: "What we are asking." Outline some specific steps that must be taken to resolve the issue. You should be clear, going into negotiation, on exactly what you want and how you can get it.

2. Use a *role-play*, in which members of your group act out the expected negotiation session before it happens. Some people take the role of the negotiators, others act as policy-makers. The latter use all their skills to defend their policy, to argue against the negotiators' position, and to get off the hook. (A good tactic for role-playing policy-makers to try is to act friendly, serve coffee, talk about the importance of "continued dialogue," but don't make any concrete commitments to actually *do* anything.) The role-play gives a realistic "run-through" of the negotiation session prior to the real meeting. It will help you anticipate policy-makers' arguments and how best to answer them.

B. *The Negotiation Session Itself*

1. Never send one person to negotiate. Always have a negotiation team of three or four. They can consult, support one another, play different roles in the session.

2. Be sure to meet with someone who can actually make policy. Businesses and government often try to turn negotiators over to their public relations people, who are skilled at defending official policy, but powerless to change it. Insist on seeing the real decision-makers.

3. Don't get drawn into "secret," "confidential," or "off-the-record" negotiations. You're negotiating for your group and have to be able to report everything back to them.

4. Clearly define goals, demands, what you're asking. Hand the policy person a written list of your proposals. Keep conversation focused as much as possible on them. Don't be afraid to raise uncomfortable questions. Don't get side-tracked. Be friendly, but insist that the real issues be dealt with: Will the policy or practice be changed or not? If they can't give an immediate answer, ask for a date when you can get the answer. "We need to know so we can tell our group and think about next steps. They've sent us to find out your position."

5. If they agree verbally to your proposals, get it in writing, along with a timetable for implementation.

6. Don't threaten, but explain the nature of your direct action group and its commitment to seeing the problem overcome. Explain that, if the problem cannot be resolved through negotiations, you are committed to public education and, if necessary, nonviolent demonstrations.

7. Look for creative solutions that treat policy-makers as human beings. Demonstrators for a good water supply in a poor area of the Central American country of Costa Rica told town officials that, if they would install the water system, the village would invite them to a fiesta to celebrate. It worked!

C. *After the Negotiation Session*

1. Write up an accurate summary of the meeting imme-

diately afterwards. Share what happened with your action group. It may also be appropriate to hold a press conference to inform the public of your results.

2. Be willing to engage in a series of negotiations if they really seem to be moving things forward and concrete changes are occuring. But don't get drawn into negotiations that are an excuse for inaction. Often one or two sessions will tell whether the meetings will be fruitful or whether moving to the next step is needed.

3. Negotiations, even if they do not achieve immediate goals, can be valuable in clearing up misunderstandings and helping parties see one another as human beings. If your goals are not achieved in a negotiation session, make clear that you are always available for further substantive discussions and that you remain open to finding a resolution through face-to-face negotiations.

STEP VI: EDUCATE

If initial negotiations fail, take your case to the general public. Here are some methods of public education:

- Public meetings
- Home meetings
- Newspaper articles
- Circulating petitions
- Door-to-door visits
- Letters to the editor
- Radio or TV interviews
- Statements by leaders
- Teach-ins
- Sermons
- Leafleting
- Prayer meetings

Many community groups—churches and synagogues, service clubs, activist groups, etc.—may be interested in a speaker. Schools and colleges can be approached with posters, banners, a literature table, leafleting, rallies, soap box speaking, college radio station interviews.

Street speaking (having your group gather at some public place and having members take turns standing on a raised area and addressing passersby) is an excellent way to reach the public while at the same time getting your group's feet wet. Members who have to speak will be stimulated to do their homework and really learn the facts behind the issue. By speaking and seeing how listeners react, they will learn how to communicate their ideas to a strange audience. They will get experience in nonviolent means of handling hecklers. Lots of leaflets can be handed out. (For more information, see George Lakey and David Richards, *How to Conduct a Street Meeting* [Friends Peace Committee, 1501 Cherry St., Philadelphia, Pa. 19102].)

The period of public education can be long or short, depending on the situation. Sometimes it can be entirely jumped over. Our Baltimore ship-blocking demonstration came *before* our "educational" appearances on TV. Often direct action demonstrations and education can go hand-in-hand. The protesters against a germ warfare center in Maryland combined a vigil in front of the gate with visits to homes throughout the surrounding town.

There are many situations in which the most effective education takes place through the kinds of nonviolent demonstrations described below. Avoid the temptation to drag out one-to-one-style education forever. Public meetings or sermons, for example, can go on for years and reach only a few hundred or at most a few thousand people, while an effective series of demonstrations can reach millions of people through the mass media and can put direct pressure on the source of the injustice.

STEP VII: ORGANIZE

Clearly, a lot of organization has taken place already in the steps above. The core group has probably expanded to draw in at least a few new people. If negotiation and education fail in reaching the group's goals, however, it is now necessary to build a strong group commitment to nonviolent struggle. Here are some steps to take.

A. *Expanding the Group*

1. Brainstorm a list of all the individuals and organizations who might support the action group. Contact them and invite them to a meeting.

*"Street theatre" is an effective way
to get across a message. Here, participants in the
Campaign for Global Justice offer a brick
(symbol of the church's preoccupation with
new buildings) to a hungry woman.*

2. Build up the list in your action notebook with names, addresses, telephones. Start a central file of potential action group members and supporters.

B. Holding Meetings of the Expanded Group

Here are some things to do with the larger group:

1. Choose a *name* for the group, if you don't already have one.

2. Get an *office* (maybe just a room in someone's house) and a phone.

3. Get group consensus on the *goals* of the campaign.

4. Do further group thinking on the direct action *strategies* that will most effectively meet the group's goals. Some additional ways to do strategizing with a larger group are:

a. Use free-floating *brainstorming* to generate action ideas.

b. Study existing *books* and write-ups on direct action and cull ideas that might apply to your situation. (Gene Sharp's *The Politics of Nonviolent Action* lists 198 kinds of nonviolent action, giving several historical examples of each.)

c. Set up a *strategy game.* This is a long process (one to three hours) but it helps large groups make, carry out, and review long-range plans in a realistic-feeling situation. It points out weaknesses in proposed strategy as well as things that work. Here's how it goes:

1) As in role-playing, different members of the group form teams that take different roles: demonstrators, policy-makers, the press, opponents, police and/or military.

2) Each group meets in a separate place (e.g., different rooms) to plan.

3) Starting with the demonstrators, each team makes a "move" in writing, sending copies to each of the other teams. (For example, "We write to the board chairman to set up a negotiation session about stopping work on the company's nuclear power plant.")

4) Moves and countermoves follow one another until a particular strategy is played out.

5) An "evaluation team" of two people screens out unrealistic moves (e.g., the demonstrators cannot say, on the second day of the action, "We overwhelm the nuclear reactor site with a million well-trained nonviolent activists.")

d. *Force-Field Analysis* and other strategy-development methods are detailed in some of the training manuals listed in Appendix E.

5. At the end of strategizing, select the most appropriate method or methods for the campaign, e.g., marches, a vigil, a blockade, street theater, a sit-in, civil disobedience. Draft an overall, written *action plan* showing realistically and in detail how you plan to carry out your action.

6. Agree upon and write down the *nonviolent discipline* that will guide the group. It is crucial that those who join the action know there is a clear commitment to nonviolence. A June 1972 anti-Vietnam war campaign at a military ammunition depot in New Jersey had the following simple discipline:

The Spirit of Our Action

Because we want everyone, including the police and the military, to join us in our attempt to stop the killing, we will not provoke them by hostile words or name-calling. Nor will we respond violently to acts directed against us by those who oppose us. The integrity of our blockade is made clearest when, by our actions, we express the love and humanity that is so lacking at Earle Depot, a place of death.

C. Deciding on Specific Tasks

1. Certain responsibilities must be undertaken in order to carry out the direct action strategy. The following are key tasks that must be covered in most direct action projects. Usually they are best carried out by a small group or team, though some may be performed by an individual.

   a. *Coordination:* To give overall guidance to the project, call meetings, and work out proposed agendas, give on-going thought to strategy. (Often the original core group plus some new people can make up the coordinating committee.)

b. *Recruitment:* To draw in allies and supporters for demonstrations and needed tasks, using such means as a phone tree, mailings, publicity, leaflets, special meetings, etc. Everyone in the action group should recruit, but the recruitment team takes special responsibility (see Appendix A for recruitment methods).

c. *Press:* To handle press contacts and publicity (Appendix B gives suggestions on how to do publicity and work with the press).

d. *Signs and Leaflets:* To paint signs with the slogans and statements to be carried by demonstrators, to write brief, clear, factual, neatly printed leaflets to be given out to the public at demonstrations (see Appendix C "Signs and Leaflets").

e. *Police:* To contact appropriate law enforcement authorities ahead of time in order to inform them of the demonstration's purpose, nonviolent spirit, and generally where and how the demonstration will take place. This may also be the team that relates to the police on the day of the demonstration. In places like Washington, D.C., it may be necessary to meet with one or more bodies (e.g., Metropolitan Police, National Capital Parks Police) to explore legal requirements for demonstrations near the White House, the Capitol, or foreign embassies. (The rationale for predemonstration contact with police is nonviolent openness and truthfulness. A practical reason is that all surprise actions tend to be seen by the police as a threat. They are less likely to react irrationally or arbitrarily if they have been contacted ahead of time and know at least the general outline of your group's plans. Also, police can sometimes be helpful, e.g., by directing traffic, letting you know of relevant laws or regulations. Obviously, however, there are times when such police contact ahead of time is either not necessary or not appropriate.)

f. *Legal:* To contact sympathetic lawyers and find out the legal situation. Do you need a permit for the demonstration? (It is demoralizing to start a march and be stopped for "parading without a permit.") What local ordinances apply? What are the possible penalties if you engage in civil disobedience and break the law? Will attorneys help provide legal counsel if there are arrests? In very large demonstrations it is helpful to have a team of lawyers and law students both participating in the action as observers and available at a central legal aid office. (A good source of sympathetic lawyers is the local office of the American Civil Liberties Union; national office: 22 East 40th Street, New York, NY 10016. Phone: 212-725-1222.)

g. *Communications:* To get together any communication equipment needed in the action, e.g., a telephone hook-up, bullhorns or a public address system for speakers, walkie-talkies for contacts between canoes and the shore or between march coordinators along the line of a large march.

h. *Finances:* To raise needed funds (e.g., for office rental, leaflets, phone), allocate them, keep accurate books, and make financial reports to the total group (see Appendix D: "Some Pointers on Fund-Raising").

i. *Training:* To give nonviolent action training to potential participants. (For specific training methods, see Step VIII, "Train for Demonstrations.")

j. *Demonstration Information/Monitoring:* To help draw up and circulate the nonviolent discipline. At the time of the demonstration, to remind people of the discipline, to give demonstrators needed information, to keep cool and think quickly if there is trouble, to intervene nonviolently to handle any disturbances. This group should have special nonviolent training and may want to wear armbands for identification at the action. They are crucial to maintain a nonviolent spirit in the action and to counter the influence of those who, for one reason or another, may want to provoke violence.[4] (In past civil rights and antiwar demonstrations the Information Group has sometimes been called "marshals," a name that has more recently been avoided because of the connotation of authoritarianism. The term "monitor" is sometimes now used.)

k. *Medical:* To handle any medical emergencies, from simple blisters to major injuries. It is helpful if a sympathetic doctor or nurse (a medical team of several professionals if the action is large) can be recruited to help with this. If no professionals are available, try to find someone with first aid training.

l. *Demonstration Facilitation:* To take overall responsibility for a particular demonstration, seeing that it is running smoothly, spotting and helping overcome problems, making needed on-the-spot decisions if any changes in plans are called for.

2. Here are some other tasks that are sometimes needed to support direct action:

a. *Scouting* a route of march or picketing site well before demonstrators arrive.

b. On-going *research* and fact-finding.

c. Taking *photos* or films of the action for the press or your own evaluation.

d. Arranging for *special equipment* (e.g., canoes for a ship blockade, portable toilets for a big rally).

e. Setting up *transportation* to and from the demon-

---

4. It is interesting to note in this regard that government and police provocateurs do not promote *non*violence. The underlying philosophy seems to be that, if a group can be provoked into violence, they can more easily be discredited in the public eye. There is evidence, for example, that Martin Luther King's 1968 march through the streets of Memphis was disrupted by provocateurs who wanted to undercut the appeal of a strong, but peaceful, demonstration. The violence (bottle-throwing and window-breaking) also gave police a pretext to move in and break up the march.

stration. (Large demonstrations often require coordination of the arrival and departure of buses.)

f. Developing *songs* and a song sheet. Leading songs at group meetings and demonstrations.

g. Setting up an *office* with typewriters, a mimeograph, supplies, files, furniture, literature, and a mailing list.

h. Arranging for *housing and food* during a protracted demonstration.

i. Supporting *family members* who cannot participate in the action, but who are doing important (though less dramatic) jobs back at home. Providing *child care*.

j. Relating to and helping people who go to *court or jail*.

k. Raising *bail money* for people in jail.

l. Relating to *special groups* (e.g., GIs at an antimilitary action, special guest speakers at a mass rally).

m. Developing *street theater* and securing necessary actors and props.

n. *Cleaning up* abandoned placards, leaflets, food wrappers, etc., after the demonstration is over.

3. Don't be overwhelmed by the variety of tasks. Use the above as a checklist. Do the jobs appropriate to your own situation. If your group is small, each person can carry out several tasks.

STEP VIII: TRAIN FOR DEMONSTRATIONS

Many people will say, "I admire nonviolence, but I know I'd hit back if someone hit me." Training helps people think through creative, nonviolent solutions to tense situations and to develop the confidence to act calmly and with goodwill in conflict situations. It also helps in general planning for the contemplated action.

Much has been written about nonviolent training. There are both written materials on training and organizations that have training programs (see Appendixes E and F). Some of the most useful training techniques are:

A. The Role-Play

The group simulates an expected situation (e.g., dealing with a heckler, being stopped by police) by having different people act out the specific roles involved: police, demonstrators, passersby, etc. The role play goes on for two to five minutes with most of the group observing and noting behavior. At the end, everyone evaluates what happened, e.g., how the "police" felt when marchers bunched around them, how the "heckler" responded when taken aside by a monitor. Question: Could the demonstrators have acted in a more effective way?

B. Quick Decision

Small groups of four to six people are given a hypothetical problem (e.g., "Someone faints on your vigil line"; "Someone in the line of march starts yelling, 'Kill the pigs!'"). The groups are given a very short time (thirty seconds to a minute) to discuss what they would do and come up with an answer. Each group reports in, and their answers are recorded on a flip chart. Then everyone evaluates and seeks the best solution. This gives groups practice in cooperative decision-making under realistic time pressure that is often found in demonstrations.

C. Situation Analysis

The group looks at a problem situation drawn on a flip chart or blackboard and discusses how best to handle it. For example, you are having a picket at the Brazilian embassy and a seemingly violent group suddenly rushes the fence, shouting "Death to the dictators!" (see the diagram on p. 141).

```
                      EMBASSY

  P                             P  =  Police
  PP    L D D D D D D D D D L
  PPP                  ↑   ↑    L  =  Leafleters
  PP                            D  =  Your group's
            V V V V                   demonstrators

                                V  =  Violent group
```

D. Hassle Lines

This requires at least eight to ten people and can easily encompass fifty or more. It gives people a realistic feel of a conflict situation and encourages creative, on-the-spot responses. The group is divided into two lines, paired off and facing each other. The facilitator gives instructions to each line. For example, to line no. 1: "You're in a silent, nonviolent vigil line in front of the White House, protesting U.S. support for dictatorships." To line no. 2: "You have a rock in your hand, and you try to push through the vigil line toward the White House fence." The group is given thirty seconds to think how to play the role, then the action starts. The facilitator breaks the action in a couple of minutes and leads a discussion-evaluation. "How did you feel?" "Why did you do what you did?" "Could the vigil line have done or said something more effective to stop you?"

STEP IX: APPEAL

This step is not always relevant, but it can be useful in situations where the action group has been dealing with a particular person or group who is responsible for maintaining the injustice. In such a case, the action group appeals to the responsible party for a just resolution. They urge that serious negotiations be undertaken. They point out the suffering that will go on (e.g., political prisoners will continue to be tortured in such and such a country's jails) if the situation is not resolved. They make clear that, if no positive steps are taken by a given date, direct action will be initiated.

STEP X: DEMONSTRATE

Demonstrations can take many forms. Gene Sharp's *The Politics of Nonviolent Action* classifies different kinds of demonstrations under the five categories of "Protest and Persuasion," "Social Non-Cooperation," "Economic Non-Cooperation," "Political Non-Cooperation," and "Nonviolent Intervention."

By this time, your group will have decided on a particular kind of demonstration or set of actions that seem most likely to reach your goals. Here are a few suggestions for organizing demonstrations.

A. *A Few Days before the Demonstration*

1. The *press team* contacts newspapers and radio and TV stations and mimeographs press releases. (If you have time, it is good to send out a background release a couple of days ahead or to hand deliver it on the day before the action. Be sure, though, to have printed releases to hand to reporters on action day.) If time is short, be sure at least to phone key media contacts. Make sure that spokespeople are chosen from the action group to speak to the press on action day. Assign someone to make reminder calls to the media early on action day. (Most press coverage is assigned by 8:30 A.M.) If the person you talk to thinks the paper or station cannot free a reporter to cover the action, see if you can arrange to call from the demonstration and tape an interview from the site.

2. Finish any final work on *signs and leaflets*. Pick people to take them to the demonstration site. Choose leafleters to hand out your statement.

3. Call the *police* and give them a general outline of plans.[5] Reiterate your group's nonviolent commitment. This may be a chance to pick up some information that will help you gauge the police response so you will know what to expect from them.

4. Have the *recruitment team* activate the phone tree. Urge everyone in the action group to call at least five or ten others who might turn out.

5. Do any final *training* of participants. In large actions, trainers may need to secure a large building (e.g., a church) where people can come to get nonviolent training to be "monitors" or to fill other roles.

6. Have a *meeting* to make final plans, check to make sure all responsibilities are being carried out, develop contingency plans, make final decisions on when and where to meet for the demonstrations. If yours is a religious group, this might be a good time to end up with singing, a liturgy, or a meeting for worship. You will end the day with composure and a sense of joining with God, "who practices kindness, justice, and righteousness in the earth" (Jeremiah 9:24).

B. On Demonstration Day

1. Early in the morning (before 8:30) the *press team* gives reminder phone calls to the media. At TV stations, talk if possible to the assignment editor—he or she tells reporters what stories to cover.

2. Get everyone together for a preaction *planning meet-*

---

5. Contacting police is not an absolute requirement for every action, nor is it necessary to tell them *all* your plans. A word, however, about *openness*. Lack of it can easily lead to mistrust, elite secret decision-making, spying by the police. The more you hide, the more encouragement there is for your opponents to try to infiltrate you. If you are open and nonviolent, you contribute to one of the few valuable forms of unemployment in the country—fewer jobs for spies, infiltrators, and agents provocateurs.

ing some distance from the site of the demonstration, perhaps in a church or a park. Since some of the participants are coming for the first time, the demonstration facilitation team needs to:

a. Review the demonstration plan and contingency plan (e.g., "If the police block our march to the nuclear sub, we'll walk to the Navy base's front gate and picket there.")

b. Give last minute instructions and answer questions. Up-date people with the latest information.

c. Introduce key people: the facilitators, the demonstration information team, leafleters, etc.

d. Review the nonviolent discipline, giving a talk on the importance of nonviolence. Hand out the discipline sheet.

e. If there is to be civil disobedience, explain the possible legal consequences of breaking the law. Point out other supportive roles for those who feel they cannot participate in civil disobedience—e.g., holding a support vigil in a nearby but legal area.

f. Remind the group of the purpose of the demonstration and its importance. This might be a time for a brief inspirational talk, a song, or group worship.

3. A note on attitude.

a. Relax. Be friendly.

b. Be calm. Don't run around or shout instructions.

c. Expect rumors. Don't spread them. Check facts and give out accurate information.

C. *At the Demonstration*

1. Drama and forcefulness can sometimes be added to a demonstration by having participants *march* or go in a procession line to the demonstration site. Some pointers to remember in marches:

a. Don't bunch up. Keep participants spaced a yard or so apart.

b. A silent march, or one with everyone singing, is

much more impressive than one where marchers are gabbing informally among themselves.

c. A knowledgeable person or persons should be at the front of the line. Demonstration facilitators and information people should be spaced throughout the line.

d. The front people should walk slowly so the back doesn't have to run to keep up.

e. A bullhorn may be useful for communication. Runners can also help the front of the line keep in touch with the middle and rear.

2. At the demonstration, the *press team* looks for reporters, gets their names and affiliation, gives them the press release, answers questions, directs them to spokespeople for interviews, does follow-up calls to the media, tapes phone interviews. (There is nothing like a "hot" interview from the scene of a good action.) Have one person stay back at the central press phone to receive up-dates from the press team and to take any calls from media people who have seen your phone number on a press release. Take plenty of dimes for on-site phone calls. It is perfectly acceptable to make reminder calls to any media people who failed to show up.

3. *Leafleters* station themselves at key spots and pass out the written statement. A smile and a friendly attitude is the best guarantee of passersby taking and reading the leaflet.

4. *Facilitators* see that demonstrators position themselves effectively and that signs can easily be read from a distance. They make sure that demonstrators do not block public throughways (unless this kind of civil disobedience has been planned). They move around and keep demonstrators up to date on what is happening. If the action is prolonged, they set up rest periods, rotate breaks, point out toilets, provide food and drinks.

5. The *information team* answers questions, hands out the nonviolent discipline to any late-comers, talks to

*Antiwar demonstrators plant a cross
and star of David on a New Jersey railroad track
to block a train carrying ammunition destined
for Vietnam. People's Blockade, summer 1972.*

potential trouble makers and intervenes to resolve any disturbances. It is important that they act as servants of the group—friendly, warm, and helpful, rather than strutting or bossy.

6. *Song leaders* get some songs going.

7. The *police group* introduces themselves to authorities, explains the purpose of the action and the nonviolent commitment, shares the leaflet, answers questions. Pressure is sometimes put on police from higher-ups to try to prevent a demonstration or to limit it so as to undercut its effectiveness. Many demonstrations would not occur if demonstrators obeyed the first order police gave or believed them when they said, "You can't do that." (You will recall how the Baltimore police tried to bluff the nonviolent fleet when it was getting ready to launch to block the *Padma*.) Be friendly and willing to negotiate nonessentials, but be clear and firm about your goals, your legal rights, and what you intend to do. Freedom of speech and assembly and petitioning for redress of grievances are basic constitutional rights. There is no reason to back down when the group is committed to nonviolence and convinced of the justice of its cause. "We've checked with our lawyer and we're clear we have a legal right to be here." "We really feel this is what we need to do."

8. The *recruitment team* gets names, addresses, and phones of new people and encourages them to come to the next meeting or demonstration.

D. *Dealing with Provocation or Violence*

1. The vast majority of demonstrations occur without violence, so the following paragraphs usually are not needed. It is good to be prepared, however, and the training sessions mentioned earlier should have helped ready the group for creative responses. If violence comes from police, the military, or other outside people, remember that:

a. Your opponent would like to undercut the effectiveness of your demonstration by provoking you into name-calling, confusion, in-fighting, desertion from the ranks, or violent retaliation. The more you can resist such provocation, the more your message can get through.

b. From a religious point of view, police and others are as much beloved children of God as we are. From a human point of view, they are misguided people who may be won to a better view.

c. Much of the power of nonviolence comes from taking suffering on oneself, not inflicting it on others.

2. If you are physically attacked, here are some things to try:

a. Stay calm and centered. Don't run or shout. Keep group discipline. Don't break ranks except to help someone who is hurt.

b. Keep your hands at your sides or open in front of you. Make clear that you have no weapons and no intention of hitting. Maintain eye contact with the attacker. Remain friendly toward your opponent and try to show goodwill. Be creative and look for ways to take nonviolent initiative.[6]

c. If you are knocked down, you can protect your body by lying in a crouched position, with hands over head and ears and with your knees tucked up.

---

6. In the summer of 1972, I participated in an antiwar demonstration that involved sitting down and holding a worship service on a railroad track down which ammunition trains passed. When a contingent of U.S. Marines tried to hustle us off the track, they grabbed people by the hair and clothes, pulled them over on their backs, and dragged them to a waiting bus. However, the demonstrators did not hit or struggle. They kept saying to the young recruits, "Brother, we know you don't want to be doing this. We don't have anything against you." The second wave of Marines, returning from the bus, seemed more uncertain. I think they expected us to break and run, or at least to fight back. They didn't expect such an onslaught of goodwill, and they became much more polite. By the time they came back for the last demonstrators, their antagonism and "gung-ho-ness" was completely washed out, and they said to the remaining seated demonstrators, "Uh, sir, would you mind coming with me."

    d. For the religious person:
    1) Remember God's presence. Pray for strength. Pray
    for attackers.
    2) Join with others. Start singing a hymn or reciting a
    prayer together. Hold hands and kneel. Meet escalat-
    ing violence with escalating love.
    3) Let God guide you to "overcome evil with good."

E. Ending the Demonstration

At the agreed-upon time, call the group together for a
brief meeting to thank them for coming and to announce
plans for next steps—continued demonstrations, up-
coming meetings. It may also be good to hold a second
meeting a bit away from the demonstration site for a
longer evaluation—getting participants' reactions on
what was good about the action, how it could be im-
proved. This is a good time for coffee and donuts and a
few songs.

STEP XI: BUILD A LONG-TERM CAMPAIGN

People in the military have no illusions that one battle
wins a war. Yet we hear people who have demonstrated
say, "I went to a march in Washington, but it didn't do
any good, so I stopped being active." The black people's
struggle for voting rights in Selma and Birmingham
took months of organizing and action. The Montgomery
bus boycott took one year. The women's suffrage campaigns and the Gandhian independence movement
spread over many years.

Major social evils and injustices will seldom, if ever, be
overcome by one beautiful demonstration. Success will
come with many interlinked actions that build an on-
going movement for social change. Before one demonstration is over, thought needs to be given to the next
one, and how pressure is going to be kept up.

At the same time, a realistic assessment must be made
of people's energy and how much time they can give to

the campaign. Often it is good to stop a movement at a logical point after making some advances, rather than going to the point of exhaustion. A campaign can be planned for two months, for example, with a plan for a break, and then pick up with new enthusiasm later on.

Around the country, nonviolent activists are digging in for the long haul. Rather than zipping to Washington for an occasional one-shot mass rally, they are setting up living communities, nonviolent training centers, and networks of communication between action groups. The best current hope for a meaningful nonviolent assault on the structures of social injustice, I think, will come from people who see nonviolent struggle, not as an occasional commitment, but as a discipline shaping one's whole way of life.

Recruitment Methods

Ways of Getting New People Involved in Your Action Group and Your Demonstrations

1. Brainstorm, at a meeting of the core group, all the individuals and groups you know who might be interested in your work. Have people follow up with calls or visits to each.

2. Urge all in your group to talk to their friends and acquaintances about the project. Get them involved.

3. Have the recruitment team set up a central contact file (on 3" x 5" or 4" x 6" cards) of people and groups:
   a. who are regular attenders at your meetings,
   b. who come to demonstrations,
   c. who are potential supporters.
Keep in close touch with groups a and b, informing them of all meetings and actions. Reach out to group c with phone calls, special mailings, personal contacts, specially arranged meetings to which they are invited, a regular newsletter.

4. Have the recruitment team set up a *Phone Tree* listing all demonstrators and potential demonstrators. This

can be invaluable in getting the word out quickly about up-coming actions.

5. At every meeting of your group:

a. Welcome new people. Encourage their participation in discussions. Help them take on some responsibility. Ask if they would put up a poster about the group at their college or organization or if they would circulate a flyer. Ask them to talk to their friends and other interested people.

b. Pass around a sign-up sheet (see the example on p. 155). Put the information collected in the central contact file.

6. At all your demonstrations and public meetings, get names, addresses, and phone numbers of attenders (perhaps with a sign-up sheet like the sample). Put them in the "potential supporters" file and make follow-up contacts.

7. Form a speakers' committee. Set up speaking engagements with interested groups.

8. Spend an afternoon leafleting at a local college or at a special college event. Put up posters. Set up a literature table. Involve sympathetic teachers and get them to make announcements in class and recruit students.

9. Have your material sent out in mailings of sympathetic groups.

10. Get your meetings and actions listed in the local peace calendar.

11. Organize a public meeting with a film or prominent speaker. Cosponsorship by other interested groups may help.

12. When calling people about participating in demonstrations, have several possible roles in mind for them. "If you can't come to this Wednesday's demonstration,

SAMPLE SIGN-UP SHEET

We need your help. If you want to be more active in the public power action group, please fill in the following:

Name_____ Phone_____

Address_____ Zip_____

Any organization(s) you represent_____

_____

Activities in which you would like to work:

__Recruitment of new people
__Making signs
__Public speaking
__Demonstrations
__Street theater
__Nonviolent training
__Negotiations
__Transportation
__Food
__Newsletter
__Family support
__Child care
__Special equipment
__Songs and singing
__Medical
__Accounting

__Writing leaflets
__Publicity, press relations
__Research, fact-finding
__Police
__Fund-raising
__Phoning, envelope addressing, office work
__Legal contacts
__Setting up public meetings
__Letters to the editor
__Housing
__Communications
__Photography
__Demonstration Information

Please list any special knowledge or skills you bring to the group:

Please list any friends or other interested people who might attend our meetings and/or demonstrations:
Name   Address   Phone

Comments, suggestions:

could you write a letter to the editor? . . . make a contribution?"

13. Keep people involved by (a) sensitivity to good group process, (b) regular communication, (c) willingness to take criticism and suggestions, (d) giving everyone something meaningful to do, (e) willingness to work hard, (f) an attitude of warmth, friendliness, and excitement about what you are doing.

Working with the Press

Responsibilities of the Press Committee

1. Handle media contacts. Make sure key events, actions, statements of your group get press coverage.

2. Develop a reputation for accuracy. Be on time for deadlines and appointments.

3. Keep an up-to-date list of key press contacts in your area.

4. Write, duplicate, and send out press releases.

5. Keep an up-to-date news clipping file.

6. Promote letters to the editor.

7. Call press conferences when appropriate.

8. Promote in-depth stories on your group's concerns, e.g., by a newspaper columnist, a TV interview with one of your people.

9. Get spokespeople who will talk to the press during demonstrations or other crucial events.

The Press Contact List: What It Should Include

1. Name and address of each newspaper or radio/TV sta-

tion in your area. Include phone number, deadline, and key contact people.

2. You can often use an already existing press list compiled by some community group—the League of Women Voters, a union, a local peace group. Your library will have the books *Working Press of the Nation* or *Ayre's Directory,* which list the media by geographical area. The phone book's yellow pages also list the local media.

3. Don't forget FM, UHF, and PBS stations. List weekly newspapers as well as the big dailies. Don't forget the news services, such as AP and UPI. They send out bulletins continually to most other media. If they take your story, it is seen automatically in many other parts of the media.

4. List as many names as possible of key contact people. Sympathetic reporters, editors, and columnists should be especially noted. You will want to call them about news stories. Other key people are the city editor (newspapers), the news director and program director (radio and TV), the assignment editor (who gives TV reporters their assignments for the day), and the producer (who sets up interview shows for radio and TV). Assignment editors are especially important for TV. They are never quoted and they take a background role as far as the public is concerned, but they largely determine the content of news programs. (By the way, the names "program director," etc., may vary slightly from area to area and media to media. Find the local jargon in your town.)

5. Make particular note of the "all news" stations. They are usually more hungry for news stories than other stations.

Cultivating the Media

1. Careful background work well before your group starts demonstrating will pay dividends. Send back-

ground material (facts and figures on your issue, quotes by well-known authorities, etc.) to a potentially sympathetic newspaper columnist, editor, or reporter, and see if you can get an appointment. Often there are sympathetic staff who will give you pointers on how to get the best coverage. Some will work hard to get your stories in.

2. To get interviewed on a radio or TV talk show, write a letter to the producer of the program. (On smaller shows, the host may serve as his or her own producer.) Tell about your group and the availability of interesting, well-informed people for an interview. Enclose photographs, a brief biography, a list of points that can be covered in an interview, and a leaflet on your group. Say you will call later to find if they are interested. Don't be discouraged if you don't get immediate results. Call around.

3. Remember that the most brilliantly-organized press team cannot get coverage for a dull or poorly-organized action. Keep in mind that reporters are looking for newsworthy stories that are of general interest (on the public mind), are exciting or dramatic (like little canoes blocking big freighters), are important, can be photographed, feature interesting or well-known personalities, or have special local interest. Seek the "news peg," the aspect of your project that will give it news value from the media's point of view.

4. If you get special air time (e.g., an interview, a supportive editorial), write a letter of thanks to the station personnel. This will strengthen relations and enhance the chance of coverage in the future.

Phoning the Media

1. If you don't have the name of a specific person, ask for "city desk" (newspapers) or the "news room" (radio and TV stations).

2. Give your name and organization and a brief description of your event—its purpose, when and where it will take place. Keep it brief, with the focus on your goals rather than the details.

3. Be enthusiastic and positive, but not unrealistic. Don't say, "we're expecting a thousand demonstrators," if you don't really expect more than fifty.

Calling a News Conference

1. Don't call one for trivialities, but only when you have some major event of special significance—the beginning of an action campaign, an important policy statement, factually backed-up accusations, etc.

2. Give the TV crew time to set up their equipment.

3. Have background information packets to give out to reporters.

4. Have one or more spokespeople from your group make or read your statement and field questions. Be concise. Don't ramble.

5. Create a friendly, informal atmosphere. Coffee will be appreciated by the reporters.

Writing Press Releases

1. Always put at the top of the page the name and phone number of a contact person, and, on the opposite side of the page, the release date and time, or the phrase, "For Immediate Release."

2. Use double or triple spacing. Leave ample margins. Start a third of the way down the first page. Use a clean ribbon for legible copy.

3. Be concise. Get it on one page, if possible. Use only one side of the page.

4. Cover "who, what, when, where, why, and how."

5. Put newsworthy eye-catchers in the first one or two sentences.

6. Put all the essential facts in the first paragraph, the less crucial details later on.

7. Have a factual, accurate tone. Don't be propagandistic. If opinions are to be shared, put them in quotes as a statement of one of your people.

SAMPLE PRESS RELEASE

Contact: FOR IMMEDIATE RELEASE

    Joe Blanchard
    Press Committee
    Friends of East Bengal
    Phone: 224-9865

                    BALTIMORE PORT BLOCKADE

    The Friends of East Bengal's Direct Action Commit-
tee announced today plans to blockade the Port of
Baltimore against Pakistani ships. Canoes and other
small craft will be used in a nonviolent action to
block freighters carrying American military and economic
aid. The first blockade will take place this Sunday,
July 14, at Port Covington.

    The Direct Action Committee is protesting U.S.
government support for the Pakistani dictatorship. The
latter regime has been condemned around the world for
its brutal military action against East Pakistan....

8. It is useful to include a photo, if you have one.

9. Use short words, sentences, paragraphs. Avoid in-group jargon.

10. Releases can be mailed in, but it is better to drop them off at the media. You get to know people that way and can answer questions, encourage coverage. Provide extra copies as requested. Make sure the last one is as legible as the first.

If You Want TV Coverage

1. The ideal time for an action to be covered by TV is between 10 A.M. and 2:30 P.M. on weekdays. An event later in the day is harder (though not impossible) to cover, because it takes time for the TV crew to get back to the station, process the film, write the accompanying story, and get ready for the six o'clock news. Events after 2:30 may be shown on the late evening news. Weekend events are harder to cover because staffs are slimmer.

2. Make your event visual. Try to imagine how it would look on film. Does the picture tell your story? Does it grab the viewer's interest?

3. Statements for TV should be short, simple, and to-the-point. They won't use more than thirty to sixty seconds of what you say—probably a lot less. You can hand the reporter a background paper with facts, figures, and philosophy.

4. Wait for cameras to be set up. Help the crew get good pictures. But don't let them run the demonstration!

5. If the program is taped and shown later, watch it. (Even a live interview show can be watched by a member of the press team.) Evaluate how your group or spokesperson came across. How can you improve for the next time?

6. Be conscious of personal appearance. If your demonstration is covered, TV viewers will glimpse your people for only a few seconds. Sloppy dress may distract them from your message or make it easier for them to disregard you.

7. Remember, some 80 percent of American people get their news via the TV. Careful work with this branch of the media is a way to reach millions of people with your message.

Signs and Leaflets

Signs: Lettering

1. The purpose of carrying a sign in a demonstration is to communicate your message to people who may not take your leaflet or stop to talk. Sharp, clear signs also communicate through press and TV.

2. The lettering on your signs should be large, printed, readable. The message should be short. "Stop the War." "Pollution Kills." "Jobs and Income Now." "Hunger Hurts." People read signs while hurrying by on the street or passing in cars. If you have more than four or five words on the sign, people won't read them.

3. Black on a white background is the most readable color.

4. Use waterproof colors in case of rain.

How to Produce Signs

1. The three main methods are:
    a. Lettering by hand with waterproof ink, paint, or magic marker.
    b. Cutting out letters on one sign and using it as a stencil. (This is especially good and quick if you want to repeat the same message on many signs.)

164

Many signs were used in the marches
and picket lines supporting the nonviolent fleet.

c. Using a silk screen. (This is neater than the above, but more expensive. Also, it takes longer to construct a silk screen.)

2. Sign-making doesn't have to be a laborious bore. Have a sign-making party with food, drinks, breaks for singing. Put on some records and paint to music.

3. Here's a way to think up the slogans you want to put on your signs. Have everyone sit down and brainstorm a list of all the short messages about your issue that quickly come to mind. Let people be free-wheeling and imaginative in their thinking. List all the ideas on a flip-chart. When many slogans have been written down, have the group go through them and pick the five or six best ones that you will use.

Carrying Signs in a Demonstration

1. Signs can often be nailed to a light stick so they can be carried above people's heads for good visibility. Sometimes police object to this, however. They have had bad experiences with people tearing the sticks off and using them to clobber others. Another simple method is to punch holes in the top corner of the sign, insert a string, then drape the sign in front of the person with the string around his or her neck.

2. Be sure that people in the demonstration are spaced far enough apart so signs can be read. Sometimes (especially on marches) demonstrators bunch up so that signs are hidden by the person walking in front. All the passerby sees is a lot of bodies and bits and pieces of your message.

3. Distribute the signs evenly among the demonstrators. You communicate more if every fifth person, from the beginning to the end of the line, has a sign, than if all the signs are grouped at the front, with none left for the last three-quarters of the line.

4. In a march or procession, put your best signs at the front. The front is also a good place for a sign or banner identifying your group.

Leaflets: Their Importance and Difficulty

1. A well-written leaflet informs people of what you are doing; it may move them to action. It can also be used as a substitute press release or as a background piece for the press. Writing a leaflet helps you think through— and state clearly—your group's purpose and what you want others to do about your concern. Leafleting itself is relatively easy, and it is fun to do.

2. A good leaflet is hard to write. We usually write for

people we know—a letter to a friend, a paper for a teacher. A leaflet, however, is written literally for "the people in the street." It is much harder to put yourself in their shoes and to think of a message that will reach them and move them to action.

Leaflet Design and Content

1. The goal of leafleting is to tell the truth simply and clearly and to evoke a positive response from the reader. The design, therefore, should be neat and graphically attractive. It is good to have an artistically-inclined person on the leaflet committee.

   a. Make the leaflet one page long. Ninety-nine percent of passersby won't read a three-page tome.

   b. If possible, use a catchy photo or art work.

   c. Keep it uncrowded. Leave large margins and some blank space. A page chock-full of printed matter discourages reading. People read on the run.

   d. Catch attention with a big, bold, short title at the top. *"Do you support torture?" "Radiation can kill your children!" "Did you know . . . ?" "Here's why women are angry!" "Who's getting the money?"*

2. The leaflet's language must communicate to the reader.

   a. Use simple language, words people are familiar with. Don't talk down to people, but be clear, concise. Don't use in-group jargon.

   b. Try to address people where they are. People hurrying out of a supermarket with the week's shopping may not respond to a leaflet saying, "Stop U.S. Support for Dictatorships," but they might read one titled, "How to Stop Creeping Inflation in Our Food Bills."

   c. Put forward clearly researched facts, not guesses.

   d. Get the reader's attention with the lead sentence. "Did you know that radiation from the new atomic power plant near here can cause cancer?" The design of the leaflet, the title, and the first line determine whether it will be read or dropped into the nearest trash can.

e. In the body of the leaflet, tell what is wrong, what needs to be changed, what the reader can do to help (e.g., write a letter, join a demonstration, don't buy non-UFW lettuce).

f. Always put your organization's name and address at the end of the leaflet. People don't like anonymous leaflets. They are actually illegal in some places.

g. If you have time, get others from the action group to look at a draft of the leaflet and make suggestions.

Producing the Leaflet: Two Methods

1. *Offset Printing:* In this method a photo is taken of the copy you want printed. The image is transferred to a plate used in the press that makes the leaflet. You need to prepare a dummy layout of what you want and take it to a shop that does offset. The *advantages* of offset are that it is fast, the copies are clear and sharp, and you can use photos and drawings. The *disadvantage* is that it is more expensive than mimeography.

2. *Mimeography:* This method involves cutting a stencil and running it on a mimeograph machine. Its *advantage* is that it is cheap and fast. You can have your own (or a rented) machine and everyone can learn to run it. The *disadvantages* are the limited number of copies you can produce on one stencil and a final copy that is somewhat less neat and sharp than offset.

How to Leaflet

1. It is good for leafleters to meet before an action to plan strategy. A pre-action role-play is an effective way to think through how best to encourage people to take and read the leaflet.

2. At the action, position the leafleters where there is a good people flow, e.g., at street corners, near the main entrance of a store.

3. Hand out the leaflet with a friendly smile and a catchy, brief comment. "Have you heard about ... ?" "This explains the demonstration." "You might want to read this." Establish eye contact. Try to reach people where they are.

4. Hand the leaflet face up, so people can see the title.

5. Take initiative. Don't wait for people to come and ask for a leaflet. Walk over and hand it to them.

Pointers on Fund Raising

Fund-Raising Methods

1. Take collections, especially at public meetings. Tell people what the money is needed for (e.g., material to make signs). Ask people to put in all their loose change. Or give the equivalent of what they'd spend in a week for cigarettes, gas, etc.

2. Sell literature, bumper stickers, buttons, and other publicity material.

3. Organize a fund-raising event. For example:
   a. A bake sale or nutritious food sale.
   b. A film showing.
   c. An outside speaker. (A speaker provides a chance, not only to raise funds, but to do self-education and spread knowledge of your issue.) The speaker can come to anything from a large, well-publicized meeting to a small, intimate party to which you invite a few potential contributors.
   d. A garage or rummage sale or auction. Everybody donates unwanted books, furniture, clothes, records, appliances, potted plants, etc.
   e. A work day. All go out and mow lawns, wash cars, paint houses, sell flowers, rake leaves, shovel snow, etc., donating what they earn to the cause.
   f. A party—folk dance, special vegetarian meal, potluck supper, banquet, song fest, etc.—with donations at the door.

g. A talent night, using your own folk singers, magicians, poets, pianists, etc.

h. A fast or simple meal.

4. Send out a fund appeal to a list of potential contributors. You may be able to get names from the mailing lists of sympathetic organizations, particularly if you are willing to share your group's mailing list with them.

5. Approach foundations. (Most won't touch direct action with a ten-foot pole, but there are some, especially local ones, that have been set up specifically to further social justice causes. See *The Foundation Directory* and *Foundation News* in your library for ideas.)

6. Make appointments to talk with financially well-off people who are known to contribute to social change groups.

7. Have members of your own group and/or supporters make monthly pledges of financial support.

8. Approach local groups that are sympathetic and may have funds to contribute. Churches and denominational social action bodies are possibilities.

Finances

1. Keep an accurate account book, showing all income and expenditures. Have a person keep it who knows something about bookkeeping.

2. Set up a bank account.

3. Get a box to hold petty cash.

4. If expenditures will be substantial, have the Finance Committee write up a budget—what the group will need for literature, mimeography, office rental, etc. for the next few months. This will give you targets for how much money you need and will help you think realistically about how to get it.

Groups Involved in
Nonviolent Direct Action & Training

American Friends Service Committee, National Office: 1501 Cherry St., Philadelphia, PA 19102. Regional offices across the U.S.A.

Churchmouse Collective, 4709 Windsor St., Philadelphia PA 19143

Fellowship of Reconciliation, Box 271, Nyack, NY 10960.

Friends Peace Committee, 1515 Cherry St., Philadelphia, PA 19102

Liberty to the Captives, 325 W. Logan St., Philadelphia, PA 19144

Movement for a New Society, 4722 Baltimore Ave., Philadelphia, PA 19143

Southern Christian Leadership Conference, 334 Auburn St., NE, Atlanta, GA 30304

War Resisters League, 339 Lafayette St., New York, NY 10012

Readings on Organizing and Training for Nonviolent Direct Action

Joan Bondurant. *Conquest of Violence: The Gandhian Philosophy of Conflict.* Berkeley: University of California Press, 1965.

M.K. Gandhi. *Nonviolent Resistance.* New York: Schocken Books, 1962.

Susanne Gowan et al. *Moving toward a New Society.* Philadelphia: New Society Press, 1976.

George Lakey. *Strategy for a Living Revolution.* New York: Grossman, 1973.

Bradford Lyttle. *Washington Action: Nov. 13-15, 1969: A Report and Comments from the Viewpoint of a Practical Organizer.* Bradford Lyttle, 339 Lafayette St., New York, NY 10012, $1.00.

Peter Matthiessen. *Sal Si Puedes: Cesar Chavez and the New American Revolution.* New York: Random House, 1969.

Bidge McKay. *Training for Nonviolent Action for High School Students.* Philadelphia: Friends Peace Committee, 1971.

William Moyer. *A People's Nonviolent Campaign Manual* (William Moyer, 4713 Windsor St., Philadelphia, PA 19143), 1976.

Chuck Noel and Bob Levering. *Crisis: Nonviolent Direct Action as a Strategy for Social Change.* Order from Fellowship of Reconciliation, Box 271, Nyack, NY 10960.

Theodore Olson and Lynne Shivers. *Training for Nonviolent Action.* London: Friends Peace Committee, 1970. Order from Friends Peace Committee, 1515 Cherry St., Philadelphia, PA 19102, $1.00.

Gene Sharp. *The Politics of Nonviolent Action.* Boston: Porter Sargent, 1973.

Charles C. Walker, Ed. *Training for Nonviolent Action.* Center for Nonviolent Conflict Resolution, Haverford College, Haverford, PA 19041.

Photo Credits

Anthony Riccardi, Philadelphia Inquirer, cover, p. iii
Keystone Press Agency, p. 2
Mark Godfrey, Magnum Photos, Inc., pp. 10, 54
Krippendorff family album, p. 13
Alex Cox, pp. 20, 23, 29, 32, 45, 49, 74, 165
The Baltimore Sunpapers, pp. 42–43
Richard Taylor, pp. 64, 77, 80, 89 bottom, 91, 102, 123, 133
Bruno Barbey, Magnum Photos, Inc., p. 89 top
Lynn Shivers, pp. 92–93
John Padula, p. 114
Steve Weinstein, pp. 146–47